D.

KOROTKOV

THE ENERGY

OF

CONSCIOUSNESS

There are more things in heaven and earth,
Horatio, than are dreamt of in your philosophy

W. Shakespeare

THE ENERGY OF CONSCIOUSNESS

Dr. Konstantin Korotkov

This book describes spiritual adventures with mediums, healers, and ordinary people on various continents. It is written by mountaineer, professor and a world renown scientist, who has devoted his life to the study of spiritual worlds from a scientific perspective. Science, Information, and Spirit this is a recurring slogan of his work for many years, and also is the name for annual international congresses held in Saint-Petersburg every July. This is a book about unusual situations in the world around us, and about unusual lives of apparently ordinary people in different countries. Measurements of health, prayer and love these are only some topics of these studies. Life - is a great adventure in our everyday reality, and you may receive a strong impulse of optimism by reading this book.

Translated from Russian by the author and Veronica Kirillova
Edited by Berney Williams, Ludmila Tolubeeva and Peter Matravers

Also by the author
  Aura and Consciousness - New Stage of Scientific Understanding. 1998.
  Light after Life. 1998
  Human Energy Fields: Study with GDV Bioelectrography. 2002.
  Measuring Energy Fields: State of the Art. Korotkov K. (Ed.). 2004.
  Champs D'Energie Humaine. Resurgence Collection. Belgique. 2005
  Geheimnisse des lebendigen Leuchtens. Herstellung Leipzig, Germany. 2006
  Les Principles De L'Analyse GDV. Marco Pietteur, Editeur, Belgue. 2009
  Energy Fields Electrophotonic Analysis In Humans And Nature. 2011
  The Energy of the Home. 2011

ISBN-13: 978-1477575994

CONTENTS

"Into this Universe and why not knowing,
Nor Whence, like Water willy-nilly flowing,
and out of it as Wind along the Waste,
I know not Wither, willy-nilly blowing.
Up from Earth's Centre through the Seventh
Gate I rose, and on the Throne of Saturn
sate, And many Knots unravel'd by the Road;
But not the Master-Knot of Human Fate..."

Omar Khayyam (1048-1131)
Persian polymath: philosopher, mathematician,
astronomer and poet

INTRODUCTION

I was recently invited to take part in a televised round table focused on the issue of therapeutic properties of water. The subject is interesting, the discussion was attended by decent people, there were different opinions, but one aspect of this event seemed completely out of place. A short story was told about a woman who had treated various diseases by casting a spell over water. She was present in the studio. The host together with a journalist-skeptic began to attack this woman in every way to convince the television audience that she was but another magician-charlatan. One of the questions posed to her by the host was as follows,

"Do you at least register your patients? Do you have anything to do with some medical education?"

"Naturally, I do", the woman answered. "I am a physician, for many years I have worked in surgery; then I was greatly disappointed and returned to healing practice, which both my grandmother and great-grandmother had been engaged in. They used to heal all the sufferers with herbs and enchanted water. By the way, my grandmother is 102 now, she is in her right mind and good health; she lives with us and still works around the house".

Such information did not fit into the scheme of exposing quackery, and the host quickly switched to another subject.

Why does this topic raise so many talks, such big interest and such contradictory attitude? From furious denial to blind worshipping. Let us try to understand, let's see what kind of data modern science provides us with, what in this topic refers to mysticism and superstitions, and what can be used in modern life.

For many years doing scientific work, I have often had to deal with people demonstrating anomalous abilities including those in the profession. At the same time, there regularly appeared charlatans or just dreamers. However, there were much more examples of the triumph of human spirit over life's circumstances and misfortunes. Many vivid examples were given at the lessons with Paralympics athletes: this is one of the main topics of the research at St. Petersburg Research Institute of Physical Culture and Sport where I work now. The Paralympics movement is the sport of disabled people who, by birth or circumstances, have been limited in their capabilities. Only through the high power of their spirit these people overcome physical limitations, pain, ill-fated circumstances, consistently train and go to the Olympic arena. Immediately after the Olympics on the same sites the Paralympics are conducted. Looking at these people, seeing their perseverance and fortitude you know that man can do a lot if only he is not lazy and is not afraid of overcoming himself.

Our consciousness has energy. It does not form from a perfect vacuum, or cosmic rays; this process is the use of internal resources of the body under the influence of strong-willed impulses, the process where the body is subordinate to consciousness and in a single impulse, powerfully realizes the hidden reserve. On these pages you will find many examples of people of unique features, their manifestations in extreme situations; however, only recently science began to understand the essence of the processes going on in such situations.

This book is about many issues: it is about the triumph of human spirit, about overcoming the usual boundaries, about what you can use in your daily life, and how modern science seeks to explain many phenomena of our psyche.

THE FASCINATION OF A DREAM

There are two ways to be fooled.
One is to believe in something that is wrong,
the other to refuse to believe in what is true.

Seren Kierkegaard (1813-1855)
Danish Christian philosopher and theologian

Have you ever wondered why poets, storytellers and philosophers were valued so much at all times? They did not produce any goods, build houses, or conquer an empire; and did not invent new machines. All they could do was dreaming and talking about their dreams and visions to others. In different centuries and in different civilizations these dreams took many forms: epics of Homer and the Sufi visions of Mukhi al-Din Ibn Arabi; tales by Hans Christian Andersen and the philosophy of Dostoevsky; realistic fantasies of John Faulz and J. Rowling's novels. What unites all these works, and thousands of others, written in different epochs of human history? They have different languages, different styles, manners, and belong to different continents. They have one in common: imagination and the images born in the brain of a writer, philosopher or a religious mystic turn into words and become the property of civilization. Why are these stories so valued by other people, why the material achievements of an epoch such as clothing, utensils, adornments and items of wealth disappeared leaving no trace, but the most delicate string of words continued to live after its had creator had gone, and after a while became the pride of the nation? Why are we, human beings, so fond of fairy tales and fantasies? What do we hope to find for ourselves in these stories invented by someone else?

Some time ago I visited the capital of American gambling-lovers Las Vegas. When you go by car to the deserts of Utah and Nevada there are hundreds of miles of red rocky hills stretching around. The great plane is seen for many thousand miles around. It is impossible to grow wheat or raise cattle there; the soil is barren and inhospitable. The summer sun burns down all living things, and the winter winds come

7

down with tornadoes and hurricanes. The chasm of the Grand Canyon tears the body of the Earth, for millions of years gnawing it into a depth of hundreds of meters, and it is impossible to believe that this is the work of a thin stream that flows along the bottom of the canyon.

It is moreover unexpected when amidst the flat lunar landscape there suddenly emerge the towers of Las Vegas. You have been just racing along the monotonous highway with few sets of gas stations, and suddenly you find yourself in the center of the lights of skyscrapers. You hardly have time to turn your head trying to grasp the meaning of signs, advertisements and glittering lights, when the city ends as suddenly as it has appeared, and you convulsively try to catch the nearest exit from the freeway to get into this Empire of Tales.

Yes, yes, it is fairy tales. Las Vegas is the essence of dreams, illusion, fairy tales embodied in real life, created by the great connoisseurs of fine human psyche. All your secret dreams, secret desires, forbidden passions become a reality.

You have dreamed about a luxurious life, here you are, for a very modest fee you get a suite at a five-star hotel which in any other city in the world would cost a monthly salary. You come to a restaurant and for $ 15 you can spend a whole day in the buffet, and pretty girls with pretty smiles will offer you all kinds of drinks. You can walk all day long about the city admiring newer and newer miracles: the live white tigers known only from fairy tales and tamed African lions; a joust on a sand-covered arena, and the most grandiose show in the world with hundreds of "Miss World" in bikinis and without them.

But the main thing in this city is, of course, the Game. You walk into a casino to find yourself in a labyrinth of corridors, halls, gardens, and elevators. You can stay there for weeks. There is everything you need to sustain your life and to recuperate for the next round at a gambling table. Thousands of machines go into the depth of the dimly lit room. As you keep walking, you can see the huge screens on the walls broadcasting horse races, battles, car races and matches going on at any given moment anywhere in the world. If you want to stake on something, fill in a form and go to the clerk. He checks something in a computer and announces at what exchange rate this casino would be ready to accept the stake, and whether a satellite broadcast of the match would be possible. I specifically checked if it was possible to stake on the outcome of the match Zenit - Torpedo which begins at 4 am of the U.S. time. The question caused no surprise but required 10 minutes of the computer work, and then I was informed that they could take the stake, but the broadcast would take place only if there was a certain amount at stake. And it was perfectly reasonable statement. This is just in the American style to hang helicopters with cameras over the Zenit stadium; it is quite real.

On the next floor of the casino there are rooms with roulette, poker, blackjack and other games of a higher class, not to mention the mysterious closed rooms where away from the uninitiated the powerful ones lose to each other their estates, shares of Microsoft and long-legged female slaves.

What makes thousands of people carry their money to the Land of Boobies and bury them in the Field of Miracles? Not all people here spend their interest earned from the billions' fortune, do they? The majority spend the whole year trying to cut out from the current income to save a little money, and then within a couple of days let it go at the green table. Why do they do so? Nobody makes them do it, nobody aims a gun at them; they come themselves and bury their money.

The reason of this phenomenon is the same as the case with popularity of fantasies about Harry Potter. In either case it is a dive into a Dream, a Fairytale, the Dream come true. Not a boring series of everyday life with work, school, problems, concerns, but a quick success, a Lucky Chance to win to change your life, to turn you into a millionaire and make rich, free. All that you need to do is to play well at the table. There are so many stories about those who made it!

But it is not as simple as that. It is excitement, a constant pursuit of an elusive goal for elusive luck.

In Las Vegas a story is told about a professional player who lived for months in a casino and wasted all his fortune, not very big but still sufficient for life. Such people are not uncommon in the capital of gambling. Some of them come just for a few weeks, while others stay there for months. With a certain skill in card games one can even keep a positive balance. The casino staff knows such regulars and treats them with special attention, even if it is just a clerk and not a Uzbek Sheikh. And one night the player was lucky. He won at the card table, and by the middle of the night the sum had already reached a five-digit number. Then he put all his winnings at the roulette wheel on zero. Casinos must take this stake, even if the stake appears a huge sum. A crowd gathered around the table and everybody held breath, waiting to see where the roulette wheel would stop. If it was zero the gambler would have a 10-fold gain, if any other number he would lose all. The croupier launched the roulette with an imperturbable air; the wheel spun, first rapidly, then more slowly and finally stopped. The arrow pointed to zero! The audience burst with cries of delight. It was the biggest win in the history of gambling. The gain, amounting to a six-digit figure! The gambler ordered champagne and caviar for everyone present in the room. Some time later the owner of the casino, who had been taken from his bed on that occasion, came and with a joyful smile embraced the player. Reporters appeared from nowhere and clicked on their cameras with flashes. The owner of the casino smiled broadly: the loss, of course, was big, but the articles that would appear the next day in all American newspapers would attract more crowds to the casino. The noise and merriment subsided only in the morning. The winner was solemnly, with drunken shouts and hugs, accompanied into his room on the 40-floor of the casino. Some girls intended to stay in the room to continue having fun in a more intimate setting but he resolutely pushed them out. He threw his jacket on the floor, took off his tie and went to a huge window overlooking the reddish hills. He took a cigarette and had a smoke with pleasure. He did not want to drink any longer but the last cigarette was a particular pleasure. Then he went up to the desk, opened a drawer, took out a pistol, checked the charge in the chamber, put the muzzle to his temple and pulled the trigger. Life for him no longer made sense. He reached the unthinkable, and it was not to happen again.

By the way, the casino owners spent a lot of efforts in search of the winner's heir. He was lonely, and only after thorough search in Minnesota his distant relative was found. In the presence of dozens of reporters he was handed a check for $ 8 million. The worst thing for the casinos is a loss of reputation. God forbid that anyone would have thought that they were involved in the death of a client.

Why did I tell it? To justify the main idea of this book: our life is chasing a dream, a search of impossible given to us by the Universe so that we may participate in the comprehension of the Great Mysteries of Life.

I am writing this sitting at a coffee shop in a French town Chamonix. The tiny town is the spiritual center of the world mountaineering. Here the first European once started the ascent into the mountains, and from here doctor Packard conquered Mont Blanc, the highest point in Europe. The top of Mont Blanc covered with eternal ice is shining in the rays of the bright sun directly opposite the place where I am drinking my coffee. From this point it seems huge and inaccessible, but last time when we decided to climb to the top it took us two days to do it. Naturally, before these days there had been years of training; the experience enabled us to choose correctly every step, every movement; the lungs captured the dolled mountain air with strain, but every step brought us closer to the Summit. Why? Again, to achieve the dream, the fantasy: difficult, dangerous and totally impractical.

So, I will once again formulate the main thesis of this book: we differ from the entire animal world by the fact that, in addition to real practical life, we live in our dreams. For the majority these are fantasies, fairy tales, novels and films. For others these are discoveries, inventions, ships and aircraft. It would seem that only a few have managed to translate their dream into reality: to become a Hollywood star, an Olympic champion, to reach the world fame or to find the entrance to the cave of Aladdin. But to some extent it is available to everyone. All you need is just a strong desire and you will bask in the sun in the courtyard of a French cafe, and in front of your eyes the icy peaks will be sparkling. You can reach this with the Energy of Your Thoughts.

"In a dream, or what? An attractive female reader asks in surprise.

"No, in reality, and achievement of the desired depends on you only".

"It's just nonsense. You need money for everything, and where to find it? Besides, there is real life, practical issues that must be dealt with, and your arguments about dreams only distract people from real life. We have to work, and not to dream!"

Now, this is the Skeptic who has interfered in our conversation. He already appeared in our previous book, "Enigmas of the Live Glow", but in reality he accompanies me all my life. He is a real materialist, a man whose feet are firmly planted on the ground, confident of his life and actively opposing all dreamers and all sorts of "junk science". "He

11

is always pleased with himself, his lunch and his wife". Due to their practicality skeptics easily make their career, they safely occupy leading positions and, as they think, confidently manage their life. But in fact it is not so. On the top of any human institutions, be it politics, administration, science or art, are Dreamers, people who by effort of their thought transform life and create the next stage of development of our civilization. These people conceive grandiose projects and inspire others with confidence in their feasibility. True, they are often not listened to; those whom they address just twist a finger at the temple. What does it depend on? In many aspects it depends on the current historical moment, the location of the sun, moon and stars. We will talk about it later and discuss the issue: how to make a dream your reality using completely concrete and practical steps.

However, let's agree from the outset that this book is not a textbook about how to achieve success in business, and not a guide to the development of esoteric sciences; this is reasoning and memoirs based on the author's personal experience and experimental facts.

HEIRS OF FAKIRS AND A COMMISSION AGAINST METEORITES

Why do we so eagerly believe in miracles?

> *Fortune-telling with the use of bones, nails, and mammoth's scales; the healer of the eighth generation from a remote village heals karma and casts a spell over water at mass sessions; Egyptian Chaldeans record the energy-information matrix of the brain, structure the bio-plasma of water and pour it into the rods of Pharaohs; the Himalayan peaks are the pyramids of Hyperborean civilization in whose depths the keepers of the Knowledge of the Collective Field have been asleep for 1200 years; The Center "Axis of the World" working under the auspices of the UN and the Council of Cosmic Elders cures from impotence, prostatitis and diseases of sushumna[1] within three visits and arranges instant lotteries.*

Familiar, isn't it? And all this has a circulation of millions of copies, allowing the noisy crowds of modern crooks not only to have a drink and tasty snack, but also to let themselves comfortable living in the open spaces of the Russian Empire. Moreover, it is typical not only for our country and our time. Magicians, sorcerers and fortune-tellers have always existed, in all times of the turbulent history of mankind. Can you find at least one generation that lived without wars, without upheavals, without violence and murder? "Man proposes and God disposes", the entire age-long history justifies the wisdom of this proverb. People have always worried about the uncertainty of tomorrow, the impossibility of foresight and the fragility of human plans. That's why we have been so anxious and want so much to believe in miracles, in Santa Claus, in a lottery, in magical healing. This childish belief helps to live, helps to cope with the routine of everyday life, to find in this life, something new and interesting. But,

---

[1] Sushumna – in Indian traditional medicine designates the energy flow along the vertebrae.

unfortunately, there are many rascals ready to use this belief and earn from it. The history of Civilization is a history of quackery. In all times Fox and Cat led the pinocchios to bury money in the Field of Miracles. And the pinocchios obediently followed them, and stood all night in the queue to give their last money to the financial pyramid. The business of the Great Schemer does not die, and his laurels do not fade! However, the modern fakirs have mastered the pseudo-scientific terminology, opened centers of energy and information techniques, and it is extremely difficult for an unsophisticated listener to distinguish them from really serious developments.

> *"In this case there were used hundred millions of the comparative forms for the invariant system as individualizing features. The determinant of matrices relevant to segments of the events, translated into the form, has the same numerical value".*
>
> *"A boundless variability of torsion fields enables him to find the desired information structures, to go into resonance with them and" read-out" useful information".*
>
> *"An excited neuron should be considered as a structural unit in the mechanism of the inter-level exchange of information and a structural element of the brain whose spin system in the composition of a mosaic is involved in the creation of ideas at the level of physical vacuum".*

Similar quotations could be cited more and more. For an ordinary reader they sound like incantations in an unknown tongue and cause involuntary respect: "Wow, they can express themselves in such a sophisticated way! Probably, it is so scientific!" But a professional scientist will respond to such pseudoscientific tirades with nothing but a contemptuous smile.

Most unfortunate is that in our time any charlatan with a vivid imagination can declare that he is a healer and for a reasonable price obtain a license from the People's Academy, and do highly profitable practice. There are practically no restrictions and control. Well, it is almost impossible to tell what is what and who is who without one's

THE ENERGY OF CONSCIOUSNESS

own sad experience. They all say beautiful words and have diplomas with real seals. However, it is our gullible fellow citizens who pay for it.

Official medicine has repeatedly tried to include healers or bio-energy-therapists into its practice. Both in Russia and in the world there is quite a lot of doctors that are open to new ideas. Healers have been invited to work in parallel with doctors on a regular basis, i.e., every day to come for a regular consultation and constantly work with patients. There are very few institutions where it really happened. Either the healers could not withstand the regular work, or the effectiveness was evidently small.

However it is impossible to deny that there are phenomena that lie beyond the modern scientific paradigm. Thus the academic scientific medium has made enormous efforts to keep the paradigm and prevent anything new and unusual. The famous slogan: "It can not be, because this can never be so" has been transformed into a slogan: "It can not be because it conflicts with science". And pundits act as priests, shaded by a universal wisdom and infinite knowledge. But so many times this wisdom impeded progress!

At night on April 26, 1806 the inhabitants of a small French village of Le Agle were awakened by the sound of falling stones, more than 2000 pieces of rocks fell on their village from the sky. This phenomenal rain of meteorites awoke not only the villagers but also members of French Royal Academy of Sciences. After careful examination of the issue they could not but admit that the stones could indeed fall from the sky.

All previous century before that event the Academy of Sciences of France, the leading scientific institution at the time, categorically denied the possibility of stones falling from the sky. "Stones can not fall from the sky because there are no stones there!" proclaimed Anthony Lavoisier, the father of modern chemistry. All reports of meteorites were officially recognized as pseudoscientific. And one can seldom find in any European museum the samples of meteorites collected prior to 1806; they were thrown away as unscientific rubbish.

Here is another example of the following century. On October 9, 1903 the newspaper "New York Times" wrote: "The car that will actually fly can be constructed as a result of joint efforts of mathematicians and engineers in a million or ten million years". On the same day a bicycle mechanic Orville Wright wrote in his diary: "We started building our machine". A few months later this car went up in the air. And then within 5 years, from 1903 until 1908, two young mechanics were trying to attract the public's attention claiming that they had built a machine heavier than air and can fly on it. Scientific observers of the leading American newspapers relying on the opinions of leading scientists and experts from the U.S. Army convincingly proved that that was impossible, and the claim of the Wright brothers should not be paid attention to. Simon Newcomb, Professor of Mathematics at a leading U.S. Johns Hopkins University published an article scientifically proving that controlled flights were "absolutely impossible". Admiral George Melville, Chief Engineer of the U.S. Navy, wrote in the North American Review that attempts to fly were "absurd". For five years the Wright brothers were flying on their airplane; and in the district they were known as eccentrics, but none paid to them serious attention, because everyone knew that "from a scientific point of view airplane flights are not possible". Once, a U.S. senator was traveling by railway. He looked out of the window and saw a flying airplane.

"What is it?" exclaimed the senator. "These are local eccentrics who claim that they have built a flying machine. But everyone knows that it is impossible. It was written in all newspapers".

"But I can see it with my own eyes!" said the senator, looking out of the window at the plane flying in circles.

"But the paper wrote it was impossible!"

After this a personal order of President Theodore Roosevelt on the organization of a special commission allowed to officially open the era of aviation.

In 1879 Thomas Edison was on the cusp of fame having patented over 150 inventions, among which were the telegraph and the phonograph. He was called "Napoleon of Science" and the Wizard from Menlo Park, the place in New Jersey where his research laboratory was situated. For more than a year Edison was developing the idea of an efficient electric light bulb. Available by the time samples of lamps with carbon electrodes were expensive and short-lived. An important issue was also the possibility to connect the lamps in parallel so that if one of them failed it would not put into darkness the whole house.

For over a year T. Edison worked on this problem, and after numerous experiments he managed to develop a prototype of the modern incandescent lamp: an evacuated flask with a high-resistance metal thread. These lamps can be connected in parallel.

When the Napoleon of Science announced about his achievement, the scientific world reacted with disbelief. The use of filaments with high resistance was considered impossible. Sir William Siemens who had spent several years working on this issue, said, "Such statement should be seen as unacceptable by science and incompatible with real scientific progress". Professor Henry Morton wrote, "I protest on behalf of real science. The experiments of T. Edison are a clear failure presented as a success. This is total deception of the public". Professor Du Montcel declared, "We must lose all sense of reality to accept such claims. The Wizard of Menlo Park appears to be quite unfamiliar with the basics of the electrical science. Mr. Edison pulls us back".

And while the lab of T.A. Edison was lit with the bright light of electric lamps, Sir William Pearce, Chief Engineer of the British Postal Union, was giving a lecture to members of the Royal Society in London in the twilight of the room lit by the flickering gas lamps. Sir Piers told his audience that the parallel connection of lamps was an "absolutely idiotic idea". By the way, three years before Sir Pearce had refused the introduction of telephones in the Post Office. He said, "In Britain there are enough small boys to deliver messages".

Naturally, the highly scientific opinion could not prevent putting into practice the inventions of T. Edison. But it was primarily due to the faith in his technical genius on the part of investors, such as J. Morgan and V. Vanderbilt. But so many great inventions could not get under way over decades, or were buried in archives.

It will be enough to mention the idea of the armored vehicle, the tank, launched in 1912 by an Australian inventor De Mole and rejected by the British Military Headquarters.

The first demonstration of a working television set in 1926 to members of the Royal Society by a British inventor John Baird was taken as a trick. Half the committee members simply did not believe their eyes, others commented on what they had seen as "nonsense", "do not understand why it is necessary?" and "What useful purpose can it serve?"

Most of the ideas of the great visionary Nikola Tesla remained on paper. And it is not just about the transfer of energy at a distance, but also about the steam turbine of original design considered by many specialists more effective than the turbine by Charles Parsons used throughout the world. By the way, Ch. Parsons, too, required more than a dozen years and uncommon ingenuity to prove the significance of his discovery. It was as follows.

On July 4, 1897, British Navy, the strongest in the world at that time, gave a parade in honor of the diamond jubilee of Her Majesty Queen Victoria. 166 warships were arranged in five rows, five miles in length each. Along the perimeter the squadron was patrolled by torpedo boats, the fastest ships of the Royal Navy.

Suddenly, to the amazement of all the admirals' staff, a small boat, only 100 feet in length, entered the location of the immaculately arranged squadron and sailed proudly towards the royal platform. Immediately, two torpedo boats rushed to the disturber but it began to easily evade their pursuers and soon left them far behind. A small boat developed the top speed of 34 knots, almost 40 miles per hour, which twice exceeded the speed of its pursuers. The captain of the ship was Charles Parsons who for 20 years had tried to offer the Admiralty the steam turbine he had invented. It had been in vain until he decided to boldly demonstrate it to the Royal persons and the Admiral Navy. Only then a triumphal procession of the turbine navy began across the world's oceans. Although, who knows, maybe Tesla's turbine design would have been more efficient?

So what does that mean? On the one hand, we face many rogues and charlatans, on the other rabid champions struggling for the "purity of science" and being eager not just to throw out the baby with the water, but strangle it at birth. How to come to understanding and not lose your head in this sea of information? Are there objective criteria to understand if it is a great achievement of science or a fancy of a semi-literate engineer?

Unfortunately, we must acknowledge that there are no such criteria. Each case requires individual consideration, and each case is fraught with unsolved mystery. The main criterion is, of course, time; and from the height of our century we can see evident intellectual ups and annoying mistakes of the previous generations. New ideas easily enter our life when the generation of die-hard scientists is replaced by the progressive youth. But do we have time to wait 100 years to be heard? Of course, not. Thus we need to rely on common sense, intuition, and professional flair maintaining fairness and breadth of thinking, hot heart and cold mind; that is a very difficult position. It is much easier to engage in faultfinding and destroy other people's ideas that do not fit into the Procrustean bed of one's own ideas.

For example, here is what a Nobel Prize-winner Steven Weinberg, the creator of the theory that brought together the weak and electromagnetic forces in nature, writes:

> *"Side by side with the main stream of scientific knowledge, there are isolated small back-waters with something splashing there, in fact what I (by selecting the most neutral terms) would call para-science: astrology, divination, telepathy, clairvoyance, telekinesis, creationism, and many of their varieties. If we could prove that at least one of these concepts have some truth, it would be the discovery of the century, much more important and significant than anything that is happening today in the normal physic".*

However, in the end of the chapter Weinberg comes to the conclusion:

> *"I think you would decide that we already know enough about Texas, that a large part of its territory has been occupied and used to such extent that it would be just pointless to try to look for fabulous golden cities. Likewise, the discovery connecting the converging structure of scientific explanations rendered a great service by teaching us that in nature there is no place for astrology, telekinesis, creationism, and other prejudices".*

This brings to mind Heinrich Schliemann, the discoverer of Troy, and the similar words which professional archaeologists told him! This demonstrates the snobbery of the professional scientists who have reached the heights in their field, who have no time and do not want to be distracted by somebody's ideas, and to whom it is easier to dismiss the ideas than to understand them.

Although, as practice shows, people who are fruitless in their efforts to create often become skeptics: impotents who can make nothing but argue furiously, criticizing everything new and unusual; academicians who have worked out their creative potential, but have not spent the pushy energy of their youth. They used a lot of efforts to get their post, and perceive every new idea as an encroachment on their private property. The watchdogs of the system advocating with bark the construction of their paradigm.

However, there is the inward logic of scientific progress, and really important ideas must force their way through in life, as grass breaking the asphalt and getting out to the sun. In addition, for each new idea the social, technical and cultural environment should mature. Some inward conditions should be created to change the scientific paradigm, and then what was absurd yesterday will become natural today. So do not be afraid of difficulties, we must work and move forward. It is appropriate to quote the words of an outstanding researcher of nature J. Lamarck,

> *"However it would better that the truth, once understood, would be doomed to a long struggle, not meeting the attention it deserves, than to perceive credulously everything generated by man's ardent imagination".*

Let us proceed from general discussions to concrete examples and consider perhaps the most controversial areas of science, the study of influence of Consciousness on the processes of the material world. This area is of great interest on the part of creative people; it causes a vicious hatred of the conservatives in science and is a field both for surprising discoveries and for a shameless fraud.

ENIGMAS OF LIFE LIGHT

God is the sun beaming light everywhere

African myths

Bob Van de Castle and Justine Owens are Americans, professors at the University of Virginia, founded by Thomas Jefferson one of the fathers of the American Constitution. Bob is an outstanding world specialist in dream research. One day we went to visit the Temple of Light. The way curved in the hills, very similar to our Russian region Kostroma. The main difference was in the quality of asphalt: Americans somehow manage to keep it without holes and ruts. What is more, constantly, not only before the visit of the country governor. Sparsely populated areas of the state were striking. Three hours by car from Washington D.C. and you can drive in the forests and hills several hours and meet no built-up areas. Only cars slowly going in different directions.

We strayed fairly long in the hills, and, finally, came to some buildings.

"Looks as if we've arrived", said Bob and parked the car.

"Are you sure that it is here?" asked Justine, "There is no parking place."

There was a lot of free space around, but in the USA any public place is first of all equipped with good parking, and its size determines the rank of the place. Just like our public places in Russia can be evaluated by the quality of restrooms.

We got out of the car, and, having looked around, Bob guided us to some large veranda. When we came closer we realized that this was not a simple veranda. A human-size statue of the dancing Indian god Shiva was standing in the middle in a huge glass case, and statue of an old man with a long beard sitting in Oriental clothing was rising on the other side.

"This is the founder of the Yoga Center, where we are now", explained Bob.

"Is this his tomb?" I asked fondly.

"No, he is still in good health, this is his copy in his lifetime", replied Justine. I wanted to knock at the statue to understand if it was made of metal or plastic, but hesitated. Americans are skilled in fiberglass - just visit Las Vegas or Disney Land.

Passing along the veranda we found ourselves on the edge of the hill from where a view to the Temple of Light opened up before our eyes. The place was wonderfully chosen. The temple was standing on the bank of a small lake, in a dell, surrounded by hills. It looked like a ship sailing in the blue waters from the top of our hill.

"As I suspected we got onto a wrong road", said Bob, pointing at the narrow motor way, coming to the gates of the temple complex.

"But if we look for a bypass route, another hour will be lost", said Justine, "So, I suggest going down here."

Exactly what we did, running down the steep grassy slope.

The building of the Temple was under restoration and covered with canvas. According to the design it should have represented a lotus. We entered the temple and got into a big hall. A sculpture with a shining sphere, obviously symbolizing the world globe, was standing in the center and 18 glass cases were located around the hall. Each was dedicated to some world religion, and sacred books, statues and images most characteristic of these religions were displayed there (see the color plates).

At the second floor we found another big hall. Wooden plates with carved dicta from sacred texts of various religions were placed in the stands around the walls. Each dictum was dedicated to the light, as a personification of the essence of God. A ray of light was rising in the middle of the hall from the pedestal surrounded by lotuses and dispersed under the ceiling to the symbols of each religion. This was the embodiment of the one God, feeding all nations with his light, giving a ray of Truth to the Earth, refracted in different ways for different nations, but keeping its uminiferous vibration. I was not lazy to take pictures of all these plates and used the dicta as epigraphs to the next chapters of this book. The author disavows himself to be incorrect: I quote what was written.

Why all nations have always associated God with light? Is it an accidental fact that the heads of saints in Christian icons are surrounded by nimbuses the glow which has always been discussed by righteous people, observing sacred phenomena? Pictures of such glow can be found in the images of Indian and South American Gods. Is this a fantasy, the Aura, or the notorious biofield, laid bare by our academic committees? What do extrasensory individuals see then? Does the biofield exist? Or it is "opiate of the people", the tales of cunning charlatans rising time and again within thousands of years? Let us try to leisurely investigate these, as well as many other questions.

SCIENCE, INFORMATION, SPIRIT

> *There is something fascinating*
> *about science. One gets such*
> *wholesale returns of conjecture out*
> *of such a trifling investment of fact.*
>
> Mark Twain (1835-1910)

"And waters will burst the banks, and will drown blooming cities and fertile lands. Marble floors will be covered with river mud, the fish will be swashing in the streets and squares of the capitals, and sun beaches will be covered with snow. Catastrophes will be following one another in the world, the peak of cataclysms will fall on the first decade of 2000, after which will slow down".

Or, in other words: "The nearest interference of influence of the given aggregate of cosmo-planet phenomena upon the Earth is expected in 1999 - 2012 in the form of exceptionally negative effects for the subjects of ethno and biosphere".

Such prophecies were made public by Russian geologist professor V. Rudnik in 2000 at the IV International Congress "Science. Information. Spirit" based on the analysis of astrological maps. Then everybody listened, discussed, and forgot in a week, but with every coming year the scale of catastrophes seemed to be more and more like it had been predicted. Well, it totally coincided in the past years. The catastrophic typhoon in Asia, flooding in Europe and USA, disaster in New Orleans, cascades of waters, whirling in the streets, washed away and toppled over cars, thousands of the dead and missing.

Typhoons, hurricanes, earthquakes all over the world. Plus human madness culminated in terrorism and wars. Bio-sphere became wild just as human brains. Different aspects of our Earth environment under the influence of the Universe activity.

But this was only one of many topics discussed at the annual International congress "Science. Information. Spirit." within the last 15 years, every July in Saint-Petersburg, Russia.

Megalithic structures of Europe and America, chronal and argon generators, psychology of communication with the unborn and dead, therapy with mineral, gemstones and leaches, express-diagnostics of a wide range of diseases. What is the connecting point between these topics, seeming cardinally opposite? Studying the widest range of traditional, classic, and absolutely fantastic directions authors from more than 40 countries of the world use one and the same method - the method of **EPI bioelectrography, Electrophotonic Imaging based on Gas Discharge Visualization (GDV) technique.** This technique allows studying photon and electron emission in the electric field of various subjects - from the human being to precious stones.

A patient places a finger on the glass electrode of the instrument, a slight buzz rings out, and a blue glow appears around the finger. No pain, no feelings. A special TV system converts the glow into a digital signal, and a dynamic, live picture of fluorescence appears in the computer screen. Then modern software comes into play, extracting information from these files. Processing is based on techniques of artificial intelligence and nonlinear mathematics. In short, a usual intrusion of mathematicians and technicians into a shaky world of human sciences. And quite a successful intrusion. All this was born in Russia, but as a rule was first valued abroad. Presentations in the majority of capitals of Europe; seminars all over America and in many countries of Asia; contracts with different companies; scientific projects in the universities of Europe, USA, National Institutes of Health of the USA. Then, gradually bioelectrography found acceptance in the native country. The congress - a culmination of development during the year, conclusions and future perspectives. The main direction of scientific congresses - medicine. Many scientists understand the limitations of modern medical knowledge and methods. Physicians and researchers had been delved deeper and deeper into subtle mechanisms of life, into the work of particular systems and organs, but then at some stage they found that the notions on the work of all these systems as a single whole are rather rough, or even primitive. An organism is a clockwork, chemical boiler, electrical machine - these are the main milestones. But a human being is not a machine, not merely a genetic code. It is a material body, plus soul and plus spirit. How to consider all this? And, moreover, measure? The EPI bioelectrography technique turned out to be exceptionally useful for these means. Imagine: a pregnant woman comes for a consultation and the first thing she does as she entered places a forefinger on the instrument's window. In 20 seconds the display shows a number which notifies about the danger of unfavorable course of pregnancy with more than 95% probability. If the number is less than 6 - everything is OK, welcome; from 6 to 9 - please, follow an examination with a doctor, more than 9 promptly! to the emergency ward. Fantasy? No, this is a technique developed and tested by doctor V.Gimbut and colleagues. Analysis of degree of seriousness of bronchial asthma, of state of gastrointestinal tract, spinal column, and all these in interaction with other systems and organs. Monitoring of condition of surgical patients after the operation, oncological patients in the process of therapy, estimation of subtle effects of acupuncture, classical and homeopathic medications. Easy, noninvasive, and relatively cheap.

And here a reader - **Skeptic** appears on the stage. There are many of them all over the world, not only in our country. They know everything, are firmly convinced in everything, and regard new ideas as an impingement on existing system. Previously, this negative attitude is part of the social system, now, only on the way of thinking. Usually they wear black tie, vigorously reject humor! (On the whole, humor is the highest achievement of the human mind. None of the animals, even the most clever dog or an elephant can not understand humor. This is purely human, and requires a very developed intellect. What is more, humor is language. Try to tell our Russian anecdotes to foreigners. Same as for us it is a serious intellectual test to understand English humor). Once you understand the humor of a culture, you have mastered the language. So, let us put the Skeptic on the pages of this book and argue with him a little bit, at any rate answer his questions. We often listen to them in different halls of different countries of the world.

Skeptic. What you have told is interesting, but sounds like fantasy. I haven't seen such instruments.

Author. The instrument passed serious clinical tests in the leading scientific institutions of Russia and is certified by the Russian Ministry of Health as a medical instrument. And it is obvious that you haven't heard of it. The technique is still "young" and has become a property of a wide range of specialists and physicians only recently. Apart from medicine such topics as "DIAGNOSTICS OF PSYCHO-EMOTIONAL STATE"; "STATES OF CONSCIOUSNESS", "INFORMATION FIELD SCHEME OF LIFE", "INVESTIGATION OF PSYCHIC ENERGY OF HUMAN", as well as a whole series of similar directions concerning research of consciousness, both in the process of normal vital activity and in special altered states, have been discussed at the congress. More than 50 articles are published in the world per-review journals. About 20 Doctor dissertations were successfully defended in the USA and Russia. National Institute of Health (NIH) in the USA have conducted several research projects using EPI.

Skeptic. Yes, we know, this is your bioenergetics. People have nothing to do, so they study informational field. It was good when scientists were formerly sent to dig potatoes. Was there at least some benefit from your activities? And what benefits do we have from your research?

Author. This line of research appeared to be very practical. Many years ago Prof. Pavel Bundzen, a Science Director of St. Petersburg Research Institute of Sport, decided to answer the question: what is the difference between top sportsmen - Olympic and World Champions - and sport activists? The entire arsenal of modern scientific techniques, from electrophysiology to genetics, was used in the research, but real success came only when Prof. Bundzen started to apply bioelectrography. At the present moment Russian Ministry of Sports has approved the "technique of EPI bioelectrographic diagnosing of the competition readiness of athletes" as a government approach and introduced it in the main Russian Olympic training centers. Later on we will discuss this topic, same as terrorism, but this is a special issue.

Skeptic. Are you saying that judging from the glow you can determine if this athlete is good or not?

Author. Yes, exactly. And also if the sportsman is ready for the competition at certain time or not and what are the shortcomings of his training. This was found to be a very effective and gainful approach. And what about the topic "ENERGOINFORMATIONAL TECHNOLOGIES IN AGING RESEARCH"? Another line of research. The percentage of elderly people in our countries increases. Soon there will be one retired person per one working person. Therefore, it is important to help elderly people to maintain activity, capacity for work, and diagnose all disorders at an early stage.

Skeptic. Of course, and then push through the law increasing the retiring age. Say that these glows become brighter after death, and the tax police will start asking income statements from the other world.

Author. I have no idea about the tax police, but "LIGHT AFTER LIFE" is one of the directions of our research, and a book of this topic has just recently been published for the third time. This topic was also present at the Congresses, for example, "REINCARNATION: STORIES BY PEOPLE WHO PASSED APPARENT DEATH".

Not only people can glow, but also many other subjects, even non-biological. However, in contrast to the human being, their glow is quite stable in time. Many subtle aspects of functioning of a subject can be discovered from this glow.

Another example, there is much talk about live and dead water. Is there some sense in this talk? It turned out that there is. Both theoretical approaches to the investigation of water, for instance **"FLICKERING FLAME IN WATER GIVES BIRTH TO LIFE AND SUPPORTS IT"**, and purely practical - from parameters of fluorescence of water in different conditions to the system structures, increasing water energy level are discussed at the congresses.

Naturally, if it is possible to investigate water, we are fascinated to see the glow of blood. Very interesting results were obtained, which can become the basis of new clinical method. Another important task: can natural oil be distinguished from the synthetic having the same chemical contents? Standard methods of research give no opportunity to solve this task. The difference can be clearly determined from glow. Then we can find how various oils influence human states.

"And is it possible to study the glow of precious stones?", this question was once put by a jeweler from Australia.

"Of course, if we had subjects to study", I replied.

Next morning he came again, took out a small packet from his pocket, and strewed a handful of sparkling diamonds all over the table.

"Here, this is for the first experiments. Later I can bring more", he said.

"Fine, thank you. Do you need some receipt?"

"No, I don't. Put them on the velvet ribbon, so that they don't roll away."

From this we started our experiments with stones. Then an Asian Indian physician, doctor Shah came to Russia. He treated patients in Bombay tying precious stones to their acupuncture points. Professor Lev Kukuy organized a clinical test of this technique for the patients with cardiac diseases at the Pokrovsky hospital. Further research proved that mineral therapy really gave positive effect. And the study of energy state of stones became a usual topic of bioelectrographic research.

Skeptic. Well, started on a merry note, but finish on a sad one. Medicine, psychology, these are respected spheres. But about stones - this smacks of chiromancy. Maybe you also studied healers and extrasensory people?

Author. Of course. This is a very interesting topic. The easiest would be to declare that this is charlatanism, to call it pseudo-science, and head a "Quack Busters"22. Fortunately, less and less depends on rigid old-minded scientific committees now. So, the healer Alan Chumak and other well-known individuals attend our Congresses, and the character of glow demonstrates if a person can do something or not. We can discuss it in more detail.

But, it seems that the reader is already tired of boring enumeration. Let me better tell you a few more real stories, which took place in recent years in different countries and situations.

A COMPUTERIZED AURA

I am come a light into the world, that whosoever believeth on me should not abide in darkness.

John 12:46, King James Bible

Once we held a workshop in a little northern city Oulu a scientific and industrial center of Finland. After the lecture I was approached by a young man who asked for a consultation. He was strong and well-nourished, but the eyes harbored anxiety, what is more the behavior was somewhat shy and diffident.

"I have certain problems, maybe you can advise something. I have done dozens of analyses, but they can find nothing."

"Fine, let us take a picture of your field," I agreed and turned on the computer. The young man put the finger on the glass electrode, a short buzz rang out, and...

"Another finger, please".

No unpleasant sensations, no pricking. All the procedure with his finger took half a second. The Brave Finnish young man had no time to be frightened. We took pictures of their fingers for another two minutes: changing fingers was an adequate task for the young man, but required time. Processing and analysis of data in computer took another 10 minutes, after which I said,

"Well, let us discuss your situation. Apparently, you have something like chronic fatigue. Depressed state of the blues, you don't want to do anything. No energy and forces for that. The doctors do not find anything and say that you are physically absolutely healthy. The boss thinks you are a malingerer. Though does not talk up about that. Everything goes amiss in life. And everything started from the financial problems which you took to heart and felt keenly. Before that you worked very tensely, forgetting about food and saving on sleep. You have never been attracted with bars and discos, you wanted something serious, and therefore you put all your efforts into the work, but failed in your first independent business, moreover because

34

of the betrayal of your best friend. These all together caused deep depression, which has now developed into diseases. You don't know what to do and nobody can help."

I ceased talking and looked at the young man. He seemed to be completely confused, even his mouth was half-open in amazement - a typical picture.

"How do you know?" he forced himself to speak, "Did my relatives tell you?"

"No, my friend, I see you for the first time in my life. ("And, hope, last time," I thought to myself). "All this is written in the picture of your field, and I just analyzed this information."

"And what shall I do?" he asked perplexedly.

"You need to get out of it. Imagine that you fell into a pit. Now you have to take your legs and pull yourself out."

"But how? I tried both exercises and vitamins, but no result."

"First of all, look at yourself from the outside. Come out of your body and situation. Understand that all your problems are in your attitude to yourself and your life. Fall asleep today and wake up tomorrow in a new life, where there is no regret for what was. The past has already gone. Return the painful thoughts to that old man, and start a new page. By the way, you have no problems on the physical level."

"But I am sometimes sick."

"Don't drink coffee with milk and, generally, pay attention to the selection of food. You have weak stomach. Drink 2-3 glasses of red dry wine and less coffee."

"And I drink 5-6 cups a day. We always have a thermos bottle with hot coffee at our company. As a matter of fact, there is such a habit in Finland. The Finish overtake Brazil in drinking coffee and play hockey practically the same as the Brazilians play football."

We talked with the guy for another half an hour and he left slightly braced up. It is still pleasant when you are told that no fatal illness is found and "most diseases are rooted in one's nervous system." But in reality it is not an easy matter to overcome these diseases! Many doctors suspect that psychosomatics is one of the essential causes of serious organic diseases, from diabetes to oncology.

How did I manage to know all this information about the Finnish guy I had never met before? To make everything clear: I am not an extrasensory individual and not a fortune-teller by stars or hands. We receive all information about the state of people using computer analysis of fingertips glow. I will later explain what it means, but now I just reproduce the line of my argument.

Fig. 1 shows the picture of field of this Finnish guy. See how weak it is, with many breaks and "holes". And now, Fig. 2 - his field, but taken with a special filter. Absolutely different picture! Powerful and bright field! No holes, no breaks. The first picture demonstrates psychological field, the second - physical. Consequently, the first conclusion: this guy has no problems on the physical level, but the nerves are out of order. What is more, these are not psychic disorders: in these cases the picture of field looks differently. Energy deficiencies shown in the diagram (inner circle of the diagrams at (Fig. 3) indicate potential physical weakness, which may be supported with optimal nutrition and way of life, so that one might never recall this. Unless he eats fried pastry, French fries, has a thermos with coffee on the table and, what is more, is nervous - ulcer is guaranteed. (For comparison Fig.4 shows how healthy diagrams look like).

Look at the EPI images of Pekka's fingers – Fig.5. The left side is significantly weaker than right. The left hand is refers to the right cerebral hemisphere, the right one - with the left. The right brain is responsible for emotions, feeling of anxiety, intuition. The left brain - logic, speech, planning, and optimism. It is also said that the right brain is female, and the left - male. In other words, all the best in human, delicate, tender, and heartfelt comes from the right brain, and all rational, provident, and strict - from the left. Both hemispheres interact, exchange information, what is more, in normal conditions the left brain dominates. It is said that both hemispheres live as an old married couple, they both have a stable attitude to life, understand each other and can get along well.

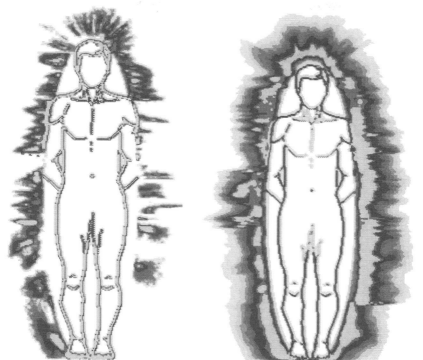

Fig.1. EPI image of Pekka   *Fig.2. EPI image of Pekka with filter*

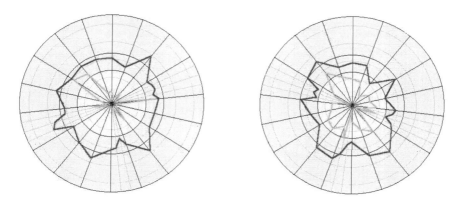

Fig.3. EPI diagram of Pekka

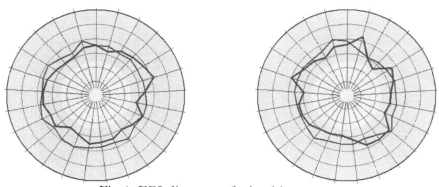

Fig.4. EPI diagram of a healthy person

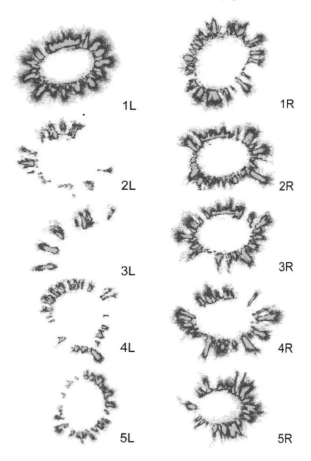

Fig.5. EPI images of Pekka's fingers

Each finger is related to certain systems and organs. This is based on the ideas of traditional Chinese medicine about the energy channels, penetrating through all the human body, but we will discuss it later. Imagination and emotions play a significant role in the mental work of Pekka (this was the guy's name). Such people are usually inventive and are inclined to invent a lot of new ideas and plans, but aren't always able to bring them into life. However, the right brain also manifests anxiety and pessimism. Therefore, creative intellectuals with developed right brain often fall into a depression. They often lower their hands at the very first failures or signs of resistance to their wonderful plans. Therefore, depressed state of Pekka is explained by the type of his energy field. How did I manage to disclose that he had financial problems? Very easy. There are only two topics for a young 28-year old man he is deeply interested in: business and women. The energy level of Pekka's sexual areas is quite active, although unbalanced. Therefore, if not women, then finance. This guy had problems in business relations.

And, finally, the last argument in the line of my reasoning was the evaluation of the level of stress done with EPI programs. In his case the level of stress is very high $A=6.97$! In a 10-point scale this is a very high level. At the same time, the health factor for both hands corresponds to the norm, i.e. it is a practically healthy young man in the state of strong distress.

So, as you see this was not a fortune[]telling, but strict mathematical analysis with the calculation of quantitative indices. What is more, the work of all programs took a few minutes, and talk with the patient - half an hour. It is necessary not just to tell him how bad everything is, but try to find the source of the problem. It can be on the psychological level, as in the case with Pekka, but can also lie in physical problems. What is more, a person observes the symptoms and starts visiting doctors, but by no means do the symptoms always show the real reason of the state. It aches in one place, and the source of the problem is somewhere else. This fully pertains to such complex diseases as hypertension, diabetes, migraines, and many other ones. And here is the EPI technique, estimating the state as a single whole, demonstrating complex, systemic and holistic picture of the functional state of systems and organs, gives its indispensable help. One does not need to sit in waiting-lines at the consulting-rooms of various specialists, but directly works on the systems requiring special attention.

Skeptic. This might be easy and understandable for you. But a normal person will never master this.

Author. You shouldn't think so. The most important is to be able to press computer buttons and pass a training course. In two days everybody starts working on his/her own, although, of course, real understanding comes with the experience of practical work. People who have basic knowledge in Traditional Chinese Medicine can do all this much easier.

Skeptic. I thought so. You have everything based on Chinese and Indian ideas, but they have not yet been proven. All this is a fantasy.

Author. These ideas are several thousand years old and they are still alive. And what's most important, they help millions of people to be healthy. You know, there is a wonderful proverb: "You can fool one person for a long time, and fool all people for some time, but you can not fool all people for a long time". So, the first criterion of truth of Orient ideas is practice. But now there are a lot of scientific research works, proving their truth. Investigation of "live glow" has a long history, and we can devote a few next pages to it.

ELECTROPHOTOSPHENES AND ENERGOGRAPHY

Allah is the Light of heavens and the earth

Surah 24:35 Al Nur, Koran

"Electro photosphenes and energography as a proof of existence of the physiological polar energy". This was the name of a small book by a doctor from St. Petersburg, Messira Pogorelsky, where he described his experiments in bioelectrography. Book, published in 1893. Many photographs of the glow of fingers and toes, ears and nose show how the pattern of fluorescence varies when the psychic state of a person changes. However, this work was far from being the first one.

In the 1770's many researchers made experiments with electricity. There was no practical benefit from this: more than 100 years still remained till the invention of the electrical bulb by Tomas Edison; life passed with candle lights, European monarchies seemed to be eternal, and science studies were mainly the lot of an aristocracy.

In 1777 a German physicist George Lichtenberg touched a metal electrode covered with glass and connected to voltage with his finger while experimenting with the electrical machine. And suddenly a burst of sparkles flew all around. This was magically beautiful, although a little bit frightening. Lichtenberg jerked back the finger and then repeated the experiment. The finger placed on the electrode was shining with bright blue light and treelike sparkles dispersed from it.

George Lichtenberg

Lichtenberg, being a real academic scientist, investigated the behavior of this fluorescence in detail, although he substituted a grounded wire for a finger. The effect was the same, which later suggested an idea that some special energy exists in the body, and first electrical then torsion properties were attributed to it.

Articles by Lichtenberg, masterfully done in German, are still cited in books on gas discharge. Further research demonstrated that electrical fluorescence was rather common in nature...

We were climbing the summit with a group of rated sportsmen in the Dombay region of the Caucasian mountains. Early in the morning, before daybreak, we climbed the glacier with perilously beetling ice lumps, and with the first light of day we were on the rocks. Every hour we climbed higher and higher, driving in the titan pitons, hanging up ropes, and the ice glacier lumps gradually turned into small black points below. By the middle of the day the sky was covered with clouds, hanging low overhead ready to rain down. Our climb was planned for a day: we intended to reach the summit by 4 - 5 p.m. and then come down before darkness. Thus we could go with light packs having taken only equipment and some provisions. Indeed, we climbed the ridge by 5 p.m. That was a narrow stone spine, breaking with steep walls on both sides. Half an hour accurately balancing on the ridge - and we were at the top. The lads cheered up and started discussing the menu of the evening dinner in the camp. I anxiously looked at the impending clouds. Suddenly we heard a thin clinking sound, like a violin string.

"Look, guys, my ice-axe is shining!" exclaimed one of the mountaineers. The end of his ice-axe turned to our side blazing with a bluish glow.

"Throw the ice-axe right now", I cried. "Guys, put all iron equipment down and pile up. Now! This is very dangerous!"

We started putting off the carbines, climbing irons, hammers, and soon it was a large iron pile on the ridge site. The iron pile droned and shined with bluish light.

One of the alpinists, Sasha Strelnikov, stepped up to the pile and wanted to put his ice-axe together with other equipment. Suddenly a dry crackle rang out; he awkwardly stretched his hands and rolled down the mountainside.

"Hold him," I shouted wildly, and together with a few guys jumped to the rope slipping away into the precipice snakelike. Fortunately, all of us were bound to one another with the ropes, and after a strong jerk, everybody fell down, all our group froze in the very odd poses having clutched at the nearby stones. We carefully pulled Sasha out and back to the ridge: he was in his senses, but couldn't move either a hand or leg.

"What was that?" he asked in a weak voice.

"Atmospheric electricity. Something like St. Elmo's Fire. The sharp beak of the Ice-axe created a disturbance in the atmosphere and provoked a lightning discharge. You were lucky that this discharge was not very strong."

"What will be with me?" plaintively asked Sasha.

"Lightning is Jupiter's tool. Now you have his mark. So we will have to carry you down as a special person with value to humanity. Maybe you will start to read thoughts or predict the future. We will check you with our instrument when we come down."

In half an hour, having drunk hot tea, Sanya could walk on his own, but all his movements were slow, uncertain, and the three alpinists had to look after his every step using the ropes. The night caught us at the rocks. We spent it sitting on narrow shelves, our teeth chattering and telling political anecdotes. We reached the base camp only in the middle of the next day, where the longed for roasted chicken was waiting for us.

I don't know if Sasha showed extrasensory capabilities, although this often happens after a lightning strike. But it was found long ago that in the prestorm environment, when the air is filled with electricity, many sharp subjects and often the human body start glowing. Is it the reason for nimbuses and aureoles of saints?

In the Nineteenth century enigmas of electricity were opening to people. One of the great inventors was Nicola Tesla, from whom we now have lamps and television sets. He invented the generator of alternating current. However, if it had not been him, somebody else would have done it. Inventions come to life when a social need for them appears. Then different people simultaneously and independently start arriving at the same ideas. This is connected with the fact that the ideas have their logic of development, and the developers shall only intuitively feel this logic.

After raising good money with his patents, Nicola Tesla began the mysterious experiments on energy transfer without wires. He did not finish his developments and died in destitution, but up to now enthusiasts have been trying to investigate his ideas. We get used to our technical progress and reap its fruits with pleasure, but is it the only possible way of development?

At the peak of his career Tesla liked to give public lectures and impress the audience with the following experience. The light was turned off in the room, Tesla turned on the generator of his own

design, stood on the platform-electrode, and his body got wrapped in the glow. The hair stood on end, glowing rays of light radiated in the space. The experiment was very effective, though not all those who wished managed to repeat it: as a matter of fact, their glow was much less and for some people even missing. Not in vain it was said that Nicola Tesla had special energy state.

Further research did not go much beyond investigations of the glow of fingers, sometimes ears, nose and other prominent parts of the body. Is it possible to reproduce Tesla's experiments and make all the body glow? Yes, it is. But is it necessary? Powerful equipment, which is not safe if not handled properly, is required for such an experiment. Moreover, the stronger electrical glow, the more ozone is generated in the air. A high concentration of ozone is far from being healthy.

So where is the similarity in the experiments of Lichtenberg, Tesla and the glow of the ice-axe? In all those cases the gas discharge appears near the earth rod. High field intensity is formed near its sharp end when placed into an electrical field. Electrons, which always exist in the air or are emitted by the bodies, start speeding up in this field and, having picked up necessary speed, ionize air molecules. Those, in their turn, emit photons, mostly in the blue and ultraviolet spectral regions. Here the glow appears. What is more, from the viewpoint of physics both a nail, an ice-axe, a human finger, and a person can be the rod. Everything depends on the scale.

"But this is certainly dangerous", exclaims the **Skeptic** appearing from nowhere.

"You said yourself how your climber was conked, and now suggest everybody should tread in his steps! Should there be natural selection to survive after the electric chair?"

"My friend, several laws of physics and physiology work to our benefit. Not electric voltage, but electric current is dangerous for the human. Current, which can flow through the body, depends on the power of its source, frequency and skin resistance. For example, power in an electrical socket is limited only with a safety-lock, it usually amounts to 5-10 kw. Skin resistance of different people changes from thousands of Ohms to dozens of millions of Ohms. So, it turns out that putting fingers into a socket with the mains voltage 110 V, one can get current rush from hundreds of milli-Amperes to tens of micro-Amperes. In one case it is practically lethal, in the other -the person will not feel anything."

I have known an electrician who cleaned the wires alive with his teeth. His skin was as the skin of a hippopotamus. Wet skin has much less resistance, as shown by examples of electrical devices thrown into the baths with villains in American thrillers.

Generators used in Bioelectrography have very small power. It means that they can not give high current, even if you lick the electrode with your tongue. In addition, these generators make use of high frequency voltages and short impulses, and by the laws of physiology such current can not penetrate into the organism, as it slides on the skin surface.

And, between you and me and a lamppost, electricity is a dangerous force, which should be treated very carefully. For example, microwave ovens.

"Well, that's a bit too thick! They are used world-wide and nothing happens", says the Skeptic with offense and not having said goodbye, disappears.

PROFESSOR OF ELECTROGRAPHY, BRAZILIAN MONK AND SOVIET ELECTRICIAN

God being truth, is the one Light of all

AdiGranih

The interest in photographing electrical fluorescence arose all over the world after the experiments of Nicola Tesla. It took two evenings to assemble a Tesla generator and start the experiments. From the middle of the Nineteenth century, the glow was first registered on photo plates and photo films.

And, when the images started to be registered and not just admired, it was found that the picture of fingertips' glow depended of the subject. Someone felt nervous or, on the contrary, fell into a meditative trance, and the photo of glow changed its form.

A significant contribution to the study of these photographs was made by a talented Byelorussian scientist Jacob Narkevich-Yodko in the end of the Nineteenth century. He was an independent landowner and spent most of his time on his estate above the river Neman. There he actively experimented with electricity, applying it in agriculture and medicine. A straight parallel with modern medicine can be drawn from the description of experiments on the stimulation of plants with electrical current, on electrotherapy, and magnetism by J. Narkevich-Yodko.

Jacob Narkevich-Yodko

But the scientific achievements of our time are not just "the new as a well-lost old". This is a new convolution of perception. In the end of the Nineteenth century, when the principles of electricity were only emerging, when the main source of light was a kerosene lamp, the

46

searching investigators were trying to apply electricity to the most different areas of life. They were as if naming the chapters of a new book, but had not enough power to write the contents. Therefore, we find the sources of one or another modern scientific direction in the works of the enthusiasts of the Nineteenth century.

J. Narkevich-Yodko developed his own original technique for making electro photographs. He made more than 1500 photographs of fingers of different people, plant leaves, grain, and in the 1890's this research attracted attention in the scientific community. In 1892 J. Narkevich-Yodko presented for the professors of St. Petersburg Institute of Experimental Medicine, after which he was appointed a "Member Employee of this Institute" by the order of the Institute patron, the Prince of Oldenburg. The results of Narkevich-Yodko created such an impression upon the scientific community that in 1893 a conference on electrography and electrophysiology was organized in St. Petersburg University. In the same year Narkevich-Yodko visited the scientific centers of Europe: Berlin, Vienna, Paris, Prague, Florence and gave lectures there. His experiments on electrography were acknowledged as important and envisaging further development everywhere. Narkevich Yodko received medals at several exhibitions, and at the Congress in France in 1900 he was nominated a professor of electrography and magnetism.

J. Narkevich-Yodko combined scientific work with public activity. He organized a health center on his estate and received people from very different social circles: from grandees to plain people, and cured many different diseases with the help of the newest for those days, methods. But with the death of J. Narkevich-Yodko the contemporaries forgot his works. He made an interesting discovery, but could not overcome the barrier which had always been in the road of wide introduction. There had been so many interesting methods, inventions, developments, which disappeared together with their authors! In order to make an idea publicly acknowledged it is necessary to introduce it deep into the collective consciousness, attract students, followers, and companions. It is obligatory to publish articles, books, written by different authors and, advisably, in different countries. Various researchers should independently test a new idea and make sure that it is effective, but in order to do so they should have a desire! And such "overcoming of a potential barrier" usually requires more than ten years. If the author has enough persistence, energy, and optimism to get his own way, the idea starts living independently and sometimes the author gets the interest. If not, then not. And, naturally, much depends on the favor of "lady Luck". The general social situation in Russia played a role in the life of Narkevich-Yodko. Evil social winds were blowing, which turned into a hurricane having destroyed the leisurely way of life of the Nineteenth century and changed the beautiful estates above the Neman and Volga rivers into cold abandoned ruins. "No prophet is accepted in his own country", especially when this prophet thinks in a non-standard way and doesn't fall into the usual pattern. But can a Prophet live a normal life?

At practically the same time, on the other side of the globe in Brazil, very similar experiments were performed by a Catholic monk, padre Landell de Morua. This was a funny little man with a long nose, disappointed in the vanity of the worldly life-and bound to devote himself to serving God. A monk's life left a lot of free time, after reading prayers and performing rituals. Some of the monks went in for gardening and sometimes, as Gregor Mendel, invented new laws of nature; somebody else researched ancient civilizations, which were all over the place in South America; but padre de Morua started inventing. He invented the technique of photo registration of electrical glow and started giving lectures and writing to social leaders in order to attract attention to his offspring. Then the little big-nose priest invented the radio (practically simultaneously with Popov and Markoni), but again he was unable to draw in large crowds. Even the military. It is worth mentioning that after more than 100 years the habits and lifestyle of South American generals haven't changed much, which I witnessed myself. When you have a date at 5 p.m. and the person comes at 8 p.m., this is normal. If he comes the next day this is excusable. If he doesn't come at all and doesn't call, and meeting you in a week says,

Padre Landell de Morua

"I am so sorry, our meeting did not come out last time. What about tomorrow 5 p.m.?" this is typical.- Great lifestyle for relaxation, a little slow for business.

So, padre de Morua was creating interesting devices all his life and trusted God that he would attract somebody's attention to the padre's inventions. God answered his prayers, but time passes slowly in heavens, and the interest to the padre's work has arisen only now. Brazilian historians disclosed many small details from the life of the little priest and published several books. At the Congress in Brazil I was solemnly presented with the sculpture figure of padre de Morua, and a pretty Brazilian woman, sitting next to me at a banquet, was telling about his wonderful inventions for a long time. I felt sorry that I didn't understand anything in Portuguese - I could have learned a lot of interesting facts.

J. Narkevich-Yodko had the same fortune in Russia as padre Landell de Morua in Brazil, as well as many other researchers all over the world. Their works acquired interest, were acknowledged, but they did not have enough organizational and business skills in order to overcome the "infancy stage" of their inventions. A first step was made, but it was not enough. Another half a century was required for the further steps. In the beginning of the Twentieth century nobody even recalled the mysterious glow. There were many other events: crises, wars, revolutions, breakthroughs in physics, discovery of antibiotics and roentgen rays - everybody was managing their crises. However, these crises were understood in one's own way and anyone who was against this understanding was ignored. Only by 1930ies the life more or less came normal. And here appeared the mysterious glow again. And, as if by chance, it was discovered anew, but there is a rule behind every chance.

THE KIRLIANS

Basic research is what I am doing when I don't know what I am doing.

Werner von Braun (1912-1977)

I have been developing lines of research connected with the Kirlian effect for several years already. Therefore, I would like to say a few words about these wonderful people.

In 1978 we got an invitation to participate in a conference dedicated to the 80-year anniversary of Semyon D. Kirlian. The conference was held in Krasnodar city, in the inventor's home land. It was organized under the aegis of "Quant" - a big research and production center, which was working on all questions connected with the sources of supply in the USSR: from clock accumulators to solar batteries. When the big international interest in the work of the married couple Kirlians was noticed at center "Quant" and benevolence of the academic authorities was shown, Semyon Kirlian was provided with a small room in the institute and several colleagues for assistance. The colleagues determined that the effects observed were real and reported about that to Moscow. And the authorities decided to make their name in the Kirlian effect. A scientific topic was opened, a popular science film was made, and a conference was organized. Owing to that work several colleagues obtained apartments in Moscow. However, in a couple of years it turned out that the first cream had already been skimmed off the milk, and in order to get more serious implementation long and laborious work was required. And that was the task of the academic organizations and higher education institutions, technological organizations, even the big ones, were not adapted for such work. Therefore, the topic was closed, the colleagues were reoriented, and the Krasnodar laboratory had existed on the enthusiasm of a few colleagues for many years after Semyon Kirlian's death, and finally became part of a medical center.

Of course, our main impression in 1978 was the meeting with Kirlian. He was alone that time - his wife Valentina had passed away in 1971. It was an elderly man, modest and not tall by appearance. His behavior showed that the walls of the home laboratory were more customary for him than the honorable chair at the scientific meeting. But apart from that it was understood that he knew his place and took such an impressive meeting confined to his anniversary as a matter of course. Deep intelligence and interest in everything which took place was felt in his slightly prominent lively eyes. He didn't take part in the scientific meetings apart from a short welcoming speech, it seemed that all those academic discussions were strange for him, but when we came to his home, a small apartment in a five- storeyed gloomy-looking building, he bucked up and showed us around his home laboratory with pleasure. It was obvious that he got used to a flow of most eminent visitors and all that fuss wasn't creating a big impression upon him. All his appearance was like saying: "I have done my part, now it's your turn!"

Semyon Kirlian spent most part of his life with his wife Valentina in a poor two-room apartment at the corner of Gorky and Kirov streets in Krasnodar. The wooden two-story house where they had started their family life was swept away by progress - a building program turned the small provincial town on the banks of the Kuban river into an industrial center. Now Gorky street is covered with brick five-storey brick structures, one of which has a memorial plaque in commemoration of the married couple Kirlians. He was an electrician, she - a school teacher. He had the practical mind of an inborn inventor, which brought him the honorary title "Honored Inventor of the USSR" and world fame afterwards. She was an intellectual, a university graduate, and his apprentice.

She was giving literature classes at school during the day, but the rest of Valentina's time belonged to him. She was his Love, his Passion, and his apprentice. She helped him in making experiments, which took the whole evenings, and often whole nights, all weekends, and all holidays. They were deeply carried away with the experiments with auras of live subjects, and since 1939 they had worked hard. The only rest they could afford was walking hand in hand under the trees and along blossoming fields so typical of the South Russian cities.

The main property of the Kirlians was their laboratory. Their small bedroom was filled with equipment. Every evening in order to go to bed they had to put away the photographic plates, developing dishes, and induction coils from their bed. The black monster in the corner was the high□voltage Tesla generator assembled by their own hands.

At night they put cloths on it. And in that room Valentina passed away in December 1971.

Semyon cut the gravestone himself and set it on the grave with his friends. Within a month after Valentina's death he turned into a spiritual man. He had never been religious, but his experiments gave him belief in the life after death. As he explained, he realized that watching the last flashes of glow of the dying leaf. He believed that "bioenergy, which produces the vibrating fluorescence of biological subjects, will never deplete, even when it leaves the dying body in the last flash of fire - it goes away into space". Consequently, the soul is eternal. And he engraved a bunch of lilies with the aura around them on her gravestone - not just for himself, but for us, in order to remind about her and him, when his time would come.

Friendship with V. Krivorotov, a talented sensitive healer, strengthened his belief in that even more. They had spent many hours together, photographing fingers' glow in the process of healing.

When everything started half a century ago, Kirlian was a local master with skillful fingers, bringing to life everything he touched. Having only four classes of education, he could repair practically any electrical appliance, from burnt electric stone to telephone. He came with the tool case and a hank of wires at first requirement in order to repair wiring, regulate a junction box or electric generator. After a number of years he learned to repair photo cameras and microscopes. He invented what he didn't know. He drew his own schemes, and spent nights reading books. He loved electricity and all machines connected with it.

These were lean and violent years, when the USSR was in chaos and turmoil. Ekaterinodar city had been founded by Kuban Cossacks in 1794, who had named it in honor of the great Empress; the Bolsheviks had renamed it Krasnodar. When the new hospital was built and electrical equipment turned out to be non-functioning, Kirlian made it work. He could handle any equipment, from electro-massage to an X‑ray unit. When his skills became well known, he started to be invited to all medical institutions of the city. In time a small two-room apartment was given to him and Valentina, where they had spent 40 years. However, at that time everyone in the USSR lived like that, and a separate apartment was considered to be a very good variant.

Once when he was repairing a high-voltage electro-massage unit at a hospital, a discharge came through his hands, but he didn't feel pain. On the contrary, he saw a very beautiful flash which was worth capturing. The idea inspired him. But how to take a picture of such phenomenon? At that time glass photographic plates were used and the captured subject needed to be pressed to the plate.

Well, and what about the subject? Of course, he needed to photograph himself. Which part? Why not a hand? So, everything started like that. He planned to use an isolating table and place the photographic plate wrapped into black paper on the surface of an electrode. The second electrode was gripped in hand, a finger was placed onto the plate, a click of a switch- and ready! He was standing on a rubber rug for isolation.

According to all responses, the original Kirlian equipment was primitively simple. He created it from the parts taken home from hospitals. Their main resources were spent for technical literature, which he bought and brought home. Valentine, being enamored of photography, developed and printed.

This is how the Kirlians described the discovery of the most interesting property of glow - dependence on psycho-physiological state:

"Perhaps, there has been no other device which would be as erratic as our handmade discharge-optical equipment. Moreover, it required triple precise tooling-optical, discharge and voltage tooling. The success of a demonstration fully depended on the experience and skills. It was impossible to keep calm. As a rule, transparent cover and optics combined in one device was checked beforehand. The equipment was always demonstrated by one of the authors, observing his hand.

The demonstration starts. Putting the hand under the transparent electrode and looking into the ocular, the author turns on the generator with his foot. From the very first second the transparent electrode starts playing up, the background is not clear, and the channels have no brightness. The author asks the guest to excuse him. The electrode is quickly disassembled, everything is cleaned again, tooled, the generator is turned on - but the same unfocused picture in the ocular. The guest, tired of waiting, wishes to look through the ocular. And, how odd: he is as if pleased with the picture. As the guest gets interested with what he has seen, the author calms down, and meanwhile cries of astonishment are heard: apparently, the guest finds something exceptional.

Recalling that the working time is already over the author finishes the demonstration, looking into the ocular himself beforehand. He is more surprised than the guest: the visibility is excellent.

This unexpected case has become a whole revelation for us. Isn't it strange: five transparent electrodes suddenly and at the same time stopped working well with one particular object, or rather, subject, and suddenly unexpectedly worked properly with another one.

It was impossible to stand such an intriguing situation indifferently. The diseased author got up from his bed and we began checking the work of five devices together on one another. There were no doubts: electrical pictures of the diseased were chaotic, pictures of the healthy represented clear play of magical discharge flow.

This is where every cloud truly has a silver lining! This is what we found through quite an unhappy fact - vasospasm. The vasospasm brought about disorder in the observed picture of electrical state."

A question arises: how independent were the Kirlians in their work, didn't they take the very idea and the main techniques from their predecessors?

The reply is very simple. Even living in St. Petersburg it hasn't been easy to find information on the experiments of the Nineteenth century, and it is not clear how that could be accomplished in the provincial Krasnodar at all! But even if we assume that the magazine "Niva" from the beginning of the century, where photos of the glow were published, somehow fell into the hands of the Kirlians; in order to reproduce such photos it was necessary to pass the whole way from the beginning! Therefore, the Kirlians could be accused of various sins: lack of knowledge of English, lack of skill to dance rock'n'roll, but certainly not of plagiarism!

The value of the recording method of the human body glow was noted by many Spiritual Teachers. The works of E. Blavatskaya, E.Roerich and Saint-Germain mark the importance of research methods of human field for the science of XX and XXI centuries.

"Each human thought, each mood and feeling immediately affect the emissions. These emissions are expressed in the light, colors and fires, obviously visible for sublime vision. Human auras shine and play the shades of every possible paints and coloring. Pure, fine thoughts and feelings cause corresponding colorings; dark, low desires, experiences and passions cause dark, smoky, muddy, ugly forms of low fires. In his aura man brings health, pleasure and light for people that surround him, or illnesses, grief, suffering and darkness".

The Aspects of Agni Yoga, 1969.

At the same time the complexity of the used equipment for obtaining electrographic pictures and its objective danger laid obstacles to wide circulation of this method.

Some more factors were added. The epoch of the great revolution in physics began. Radio-activity and X-rays and "the tiniest particle of substance'", electron, had been just discovered; heated disputes concerning the theory of Maxwell electromagnetic fields were still in full swing, not far off there was Einstein's revolution in physics. At the same time, these years were noted by the growing interest to abnormal manifestations of human nature. Calling the spirits of the dead was practiced all over the world; E. Blavatskaya created theosophy; mystics and occultists of different kinds attracted wide attention. Therefore the new method that enabled to record the changes of mental energy caused wide interest in their environment, which led to a loss of interest of and tearing away from the academic circles. Thus, the basic advantage of the method played with it a malicious joke: the end of XIX century was an obviously adverse environment for it. Some publications, such as the book by Messira Pogorelsky "Electro-photosphens and energography as a proof of existence of physiological polar energy", 1899, only aggravated the situation. After Ya. O. Narkevich-Jodko's death in 1905 and new revolutionary situations in physics and the society, the works of the founders of bioelectrography were for a long time forgotten, and we consider them now as the historical predecessors of the Kirlians.

Several dozens years the Kirlians were engaged in development and improvement of their creation, investigating the glow characteristics of more and more different materials. They received more than 30 certificates on inventions, and in 1974 Simeon Davydovich was given the deserved title of the "Honorary Inventor of the USSR". And it is not so important that later in old journals similar photos made in the end of the last century were found; the name "Kirlian Effect" had been already recognized worldwide. Further there were attempts to give this phenomenon other names: each researcher who obtained more or less interesting results with the use of any updating of the Kirlian effect immediately declared his study a new phenomenon and gave it his name, however studies of physical processes of image formation showed that with all the variety of electrodes and voltages the essence of the proceeding processes remains the same.

Again the same situation repeats in history: a phenomenon is given the name of the one who most vividly and in proper time informed the world about it. America was discovered by Vikings, Columbus cleared a road to it, but it was named after Amerigo Vespucci. Therefore it is reasonable to introduce various terms for scientific use, differently to designate various updates, but the common name of the method should remain without changes, the **KIRLIAN EFFECT**.

In the majority of books about the effect, it was related to abnormal phenomena of human mentality, and from the very beginning the issue had a certain touch of mysticism. It was possible to find the explanations that were, on the one hand, rather far from the scientific paradigm, such as manifestation of cosmic energy, or emanation of energy of the Deity on human fingers. On the other hand, there were articles showing that the named effect is nothing more than changes in perspiration. As it often happens, the Truth was somewhere in the middle.

The Kirlians

INDEX OF HEALTH

> *In the effulgent lotus of the heart dwells*
> *Brahman the Light of lights*
>
> *Upanishad*

I have a friend, a professor of our University. He is a very energetic person, hale and hearty, and self confident. He can tell about his projects, problems, and beloved women for hours, and the interlocutor needs to just show minimum attention: he has his own opinion about everything. From time to time Arkady (that's how I call him; students, respectively, Arkady Valentinovich) comes to our laboratory to drink tea and speak about his plans. And to admire his own perfect and bright field. It usually looks as a model (Fig. 6).

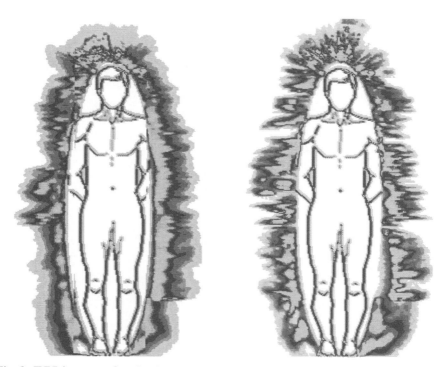

Fig.6. EPI image of Arkady   *Fig.7. EPI image of Arkady next day*

But once he came, and the field was much weaker: (Fig. 7)

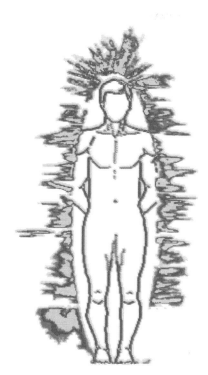

Arkady was surprised and advised to check our equipment. In order to test the instruments we usually take images of a special titanium cylinder and use this data to determine the stability of work. Everything was in order. Next day the field was even worse (Fig. 8)

Arkady felt very well, so for the whole hour with the wit typical of our intellectuals he was describing what benefit we could have brought to our country and all of Humanity if we had given up our field and had started doing something useful, for example, growing spring onions.

The next day he got a serious flu and spent a week in bed with high temperature.

Fig.8. EPI image of Arkady day after

Such situations are not rare. All potential problems first of all show up in the field picture. These can be temporary functional disorders, which pass quickly and don't leave vestiges, or more constant disorders, which arise as a result of permanent negative factors: bad ecology, wrong nutrition, emotional experiences, stress, or other people's negative fields. The human energy field becomes disrupted, defective, which opens up additional opportunities for harmful agents to penetrate. And in some moment a functionally weak and overloaded system doesn't stand, and the problem passes to the physical level. The person gets ill - symptoms appear.

It is particularly apparent with children. Children's field is very active and unsteady, same as children's mood: if a child disconsolately cries, amuse him - and in a minute he starts laughing merrily. Thus the field, especially psychological, changes several times during the day, reflecting intensive character of information exchange of the child with the environment. At the beginning this fact put us at a nonplus. How should we work with children? How should we make their analysis? As far as we accumulated experience together with pediatricians it became clear that the picture which we observed on the computer screen was the reflection of the real psychophysiological situation. Indeed, the child's field changes, but this is the reflection of real processes. And if some special marks like such "double rings" around fingers appear in the field picture (Fig. 9) this indicates the altered state of psyche, caused by some specific conditions, and in many cases, unfortunately, by drugs.

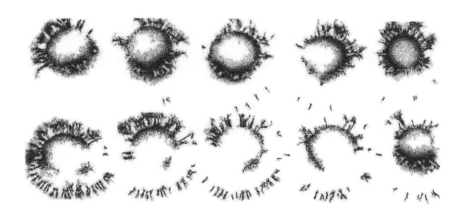

Fig.9. Indications of the altered state of psyche

At the same time, it was found that the picture of a healthy child with filter should fully meet general rules: i.e. be even and bright. Deviations indicate the present or potential problems with health. Or, in other words, functional disorders. This picture is more stable for adults, for children it changes with the change of functional state, but all in all it doesn't lose its diagnostic meaning.

Sasha was a normal, well developed 5-year-old child. He attended kindergarten, sometimes had childhood diseases: fevers, scarlatina, cold in the head. The only thing which worried his parents was his periodic state when Sasha would lie down and say that he had "no power to move". He lay for half an hour, and then ran to play again. Parents brought Sasha to doctors, made different analysis - everything was more or less normal. Then they came to take a picture of his field with filter - it was all disrupted and weak. It was unclear which particular systems are connected with this. Some general system disorder. Pictures of parents' field were taken: (Fig. 10,11).

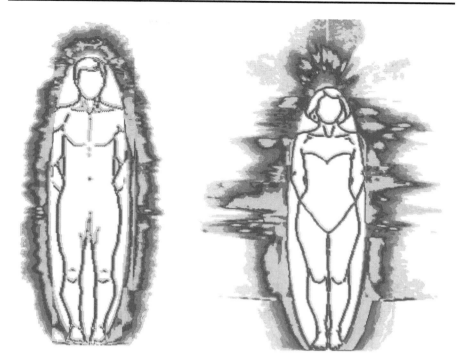

Fig.10. EPI image of a father   *Fig.11. EPI image of a mother*

Father had dense and closed field, as a turtle's shell, mother's field was powerful and super active. Our psychologist spoke with the parents. Father - a typical engineer, worked in a state organization, with a lot of responsibilities, very low salary put into his card, so as not to feel ashamed of one another coming for salary. The mother - a new Russian (nouveaux riche) business woman, who managed a publishing house, and her husband and son. These people always have a special type of field: they spread it in the space as tentacles, actively influencing all surrounding people. Naturally, no time for family life and playing with the child. We advised to somehow change the situation: to change the way they treated the child and to revise his nutrition. It would be cheaper to hire a nurse, or father had to quit work. The mother listened silently, thanked and left. Nothing really was done. In two months Sasha's blood formula significantly changed, though before that his analyses had been quite good. He was taken to hospital and treated, but in our opinion the reason of the disease was not on the physical, but on the psychological level.

Such impressions led us with Prof. Pavel Bundzen to the creation of "health index." - index, which would characterize the human state as temperature and blood pressure. 36.6^{0}C $(98^{0}$F$)$ - everything is OK, 37.0^{0}C $(99^{0}$F$)$ - some flaccid inflammatory process in the organism, 38.0^{0}C $(100^{0}$F$)$ - already a disease. The biofield's picture has the same peculiarities. Individual features are present, but there is something common. How to describe this? After long experiments and discussions with Prof. Bundzen we came to the conclusion that such index is the integral coefficient, calculated in the "EPI Diagram" program.

I will not bother you with the description of how this coefficient is calculated. You can find this in our publications . In order to test our idea we asked all our colleagues to measure healthy people and send us the results. Many people replied and in a month we had a database of practically healthy people from Sweden, Germany, USA, and, certainly, Russia.

Skeptic. And how did you know that they were healthy? Did you have results of blood, urine analyses, clinical trials?

Author. No, we did not have that in most of the cases. Clinical trials require several days, a group of specialists and equipment. Therefore, we are speaking about "practically healthy" people, i.e. people who had no serious diseases or, as usual, chronic problems compensated at the expense of other physiological systems. As soon as the data was gathered, statistics began to work: the calculated integral coefficients formed certain domain for the majority of people. This domain was taken as normal based on the laws of statistics. What was more, the size of this domain depended on the age. The ratio between the coefficients of right and left hands characterized balance of brain hemispheres.

Skeptic. And where did you take this from?

Author. This is one of the results of our long term research, and we will discuss it next time.

Skeptic. What for do you need this index? Where can you use it?

Author. Once we participated in the examination of people from the Chernobyl zone. A first problem which arose for medical commissions who came to carry out examination: what specialists should be taken and what analysis should be made? The budget was always limited, a great number of people should be examined, and nobody had any idea about their health. Here the index of health was right to the point. It allowed making selection at the first stage: when the person was healthy or when the state of the organism required attention. In the first case a person should go home, and in the second - the analysis should be made and specialists should be consulted.

Mass medical examination at school, at work, in the army has the same goal. But in the everyday life the index of health plays an important role. An example from my practice.

June and July is a very tight time in our work. Completing and handing over reports, preparing and holding the Congress, a couple of workshops - work 12 hours a day 7 days a week. Therefore, I was not surprised when my EPI images became very bad in the middle of July. "OK, the Congress will end, everybody will leave, I will have a chance to peacefully sit in my summer house, make conclusions, prepare a few articles, and everything will improve", I consoled myself. What was more; it was hard to assess some particular systems and organs: the field became entirely small, the EPI diagram "shrank" and mostly passed into the negative area.

August came, I could have peaceful rest, sitting at the computer, my physical state seemed to be normal, but EPI images did not revert to the norm.

And on August 5 (I can remember it was Saturday) what I felt was like a splinter in a heel. Examined - nothing was seen. Just in case, swabbed with iodine. I was scalded with pain as if with boiling water and temperature rose by Sunday night. Then from bad to worse. Abscess, lymphadenitis, temperature. It resulted in two surgeries, a week in hospital and three weeks of out-patient treatment. It became clear to me how Bazarov from Turgeniev's novel "Fathers and Sons" could have died of cutting a finger. Now we have antibiotics, plasma-foresees, blood photo-modification, and what was then? Only bloodletting and a priest.

This entire unpleasant situation was first of all connected with general weakening of the organism, loss of immunity, as well as with the ingress of some foreign agents. Could that have been determined beforehand using standard methods? Theoretically, yes. Practically - no. Identification of immune status by blood is quite a complex and expensive analysis. EPI bioelectrography method enabled to easily and quickly determine that the index of health fell lower than the norm. What can be done in this case? First of all, it's necessary to increase the energy level. Not to look for the cause of energy deficiency, to take the necessary steps right away. The best I could have done was to go somewhere to the mountains for a week, walk mountain tracks and drink glacial water. If this was not possible, to use the system of complex immunocorrection. If it did not help - look for the cause of energy deficiency, not waiting until the disease developed. And another thing, very important - to meditate, pray and try to understand what is wrong in your life, what is your sin in the face of God.

By the way, after treatment my EPI images came back to normal. But still it was necessary to go to the mountains.

Thus, evaluation of the index of health represents a new approach to the control of state. Correction of the state of an individual, not treatment of the diseases. Let us avoid bringing ourselves to disease. Let us support our body and soul in active working state.

"Who needs this?" you will ask. Each of us! In order to be healthy, cheerful and full of energy, not to get into hospital breaking all life plans and then to earn money for pills during half of your life, not to loose life tonus and correct brewing problems when convenient for you.

I believe that in some time systems of monitoring and long term control of health state on computer basis will start being actively developed in the world. Use a device once a day, place your hand, the device takes a set of parameters and sends to the Internet database. One can always take this device along. Parameters are in the normal range - everything is OK. Beyond the normal limits - and nice lady's voice warns you: "Mr. Johnson, please, pay attention to your liver. Refrain from the third glass of wine". Parameters are in the dangerous zone - a signal to the doctor: detailed analyses should be made. Thus a disease can be caught at the very early stage, and this makes doctor's work considerably easier: modern medicine effectively copes with the early stage diseases, perfect when no clinical symptoms.

Our colleagues from the Ukrainian city Dnepropetrovsk told about two similar cases with different consequences. In both cases the field picture indicated strong blocks in the head area. Both persons were healthy active men about 50 years old. One of them listened to the advice of doctors, visited massage, started doing exercises and taking natural measures. The picture improved in a month, and then it was entirely in the norm zone. The second client did not believe gave up on the doctors: "Cooking up here". In a month he had a stroke, was hospitalized and partially lost his brain activity. The main principle of preventive medicine - to find out potentially dangerous zones of physical symptoms and correct the disorders using the most natural methods. Of course, we are doing only first steps on the way of preventive medicine, and many questions require understanding. For example, the following case happened not long ago. A man of about 40 years old. We measured the field - a low index of health. Nothing particular was found. We advised to take a rest and eat vegetables and fruit. In a few days he pricked a finger with a bone. Next day - temperature 39°C and a very serious inflammation. A month in the hospital. We are speaking about weakening of immunity, but in the majority of cases these are just words. Bioelectrography technique enables to quickly and easily evaluate the index of health, field picture, and, thus, estimate the general state. This data can be transferred to the central database by Internet, where it will be stored during the whole person's life.

Skeptic. And what about personal data secret? Each hacker will be able to get into the Internet and download your data. And then a person will not be employed because his field is crooked. This smells of total surveillance.

Author. As if now it is impossible to go to the hospital and take the health history of any person! A little bit of persistency - and you got it. But on the other hand, you are right: information society requires more and more openness from every person. Individual number, tax history, credit history, insurance history, car insurance. There are a lot of advantages in this, although certain inconveniences. Western society becomes open. No choice but to hope for the development of improved collective mind. Later on we will discuss this.

OUT OF BODY EXPERIENCE AND OTHER TRANSFORMATIONS OF AURA

The light of Wakan Tanka is upon my people

Kablaya

In the middle of 1960's a book by Robert Monroe "Journeys out of the Body" was published in the USA. It described feelings of the author whose spirit separated from the body and began to travel in space independently. At first it scared him very much and he tried to come back into his body. Gradually, as he made sure that nothing fearful went on, he started making his spiritual travels longer and not just looking at his body at rest from the outside, but flying away from it quite far. As mentioned by Monroe, he could fly through the walls, visit people's houses, known and unknown places, in short, take up good tourism without any inconveniences for the physical body and bank account. Monroe even developed a technique of learning to travel outside of their physical body for everyone who wishes.

The book became well-known on the West, there appeared researchers, scientists determined that the process of leaving the body is similar to autohypnosis, and the brain really passes into some special state, which is different from both wakeful state and sleep.

Robert Monroe was a talented person. He had an enterprising spirit typical of an American. He managed to create a school featuring his technique, started a journal and published audio cassettes and books. As he began to be successful he eventually created his own institute. The important achievement of this institute was that they discovered the fact that certain low frequency sound signals given through earphones stimulate transition into the state of spiritual travel. Monroe passed away in 1987 however his institute continues to work successfully. So, being in Virginia, I agreed to Bob Van de Castle's offer to visit this institution.

After breakfast we got into the car and drove through the forest expanses of Virginia. The first item on our agenda was a visit to the Buddhist Center. The prior of this Center, lama Tenzin, had been present at my lecture and had invited us to visit his estates. After an hour travel we left the main road and turned onto a dirt road. At once I recalled our bad motorways in Russia, as even the dirty roads were well-made in Virginia, without deep holes and ruts. We used to say that there are no motorways in Russia, only directions. We crossed the river and, having gone up the hill, entered the gates of the Buddhist Center. Parking proved to be quite good there.

The Center occupied a wonderful place: on top of the hill, surrounded by wooded slopes with branchy trees. Virginia is situated in the same latitude as Turkey, and it is quite hot there in summer. The original occupation of Virginian gentlemen was growing tobacco, and until now, notwithstanding all American anti-smoking campaign, you can see tobacco plantations in some places. All over the country there are a lot of forests, and American white-tail deer bravely come to the road, and squirrels sincerely think that the human being is a kind of source of nuts.

Lama Tenzin was very young, about 30 years by appearance, but it is very difficult for us to determine the age of the Tibetans. Most of his life he had spent in India, had got good education, and 12 years ago had been sent to the USA by the Dalai Lama, in order to preach Tibetan Buddhism.

What a paradoxical situation: the Chinese had captured Tibet, had destroyed hundreds of monasteries, thousands of monks. The Dalai Lama had had to escape to India. A horrible harm had been done against peaceful, friendly people. The world had condemned this deed, but nothing had been done. Even in our days people with slogans "Freedom for Tibet" walk around the Trafalgar Column in London - but what's the sense? And as a result of those political processes, the once fully closed and secret schools of Tibetan Buddhism have begun to spread in the world. Tibetan sacred books were translated into European languages, their interpretations and liberal translations appeared. It has turned out that Buddhist philosophy with its peaceful acceptance of good and evil, fundamental attitude to death, inner spiritual essence of human being as the basis, has greatly contributed to teaching the soul of Western people. European interpreters of sacred texts have appeared, but they haven't managed to always penetrate into the core of the ancient teachings themselves. Therefore, the Dalai Lama constantly sends his emissaries to the world and spends a lot of time outside India himself. An interesting question: if the Chinese had not captured Tibet, would this secret religion have become widespread in the world, or would it have remained behind the ice barriers of the mountains? What is Good and Evil in this world? Isn't Devil the antithesis of God, created by God not to let God to become too proud for the results of his work? Evil makes a step, so that God could come forward and show itself. There is no place for development in perfect world with absolute balance.

Tenzin managed to justify the hopes of the Dalai Lama. He created centers in USA, Mexico, Poland, and Russia. He wrote a number of good books and published them in different languages, including Russian. Hundreds of people gather at his Center in the Virginian hills for workshops, festivals, and holidays. They come together with their families, children, friends, and many of them find a cozy spiritual place there. You don't have to say you are a Buddhist to come there. People of all races, nations, and religions are accepted in the Center.

Tenzin guided us around the territory of the Center, showed halls for meetings and meditations, educational center, and the hotel under construction. After that we had a nice vegeterian lunch and pleasant discussion on the open veranda. The food was tasty, healthy, from natural plants and vegetables, and this was a pleasant exception of a typical American ration. (The fact is that from a European point of view usual American food is tasteless, synthetic, and not as healthy. This nation suffers from many diseases, first of all, because of the character of their usual nutrition. But the topic of healthy nutrition we will discuss another time). We left the Center of Tenzin in a most wonderful mood. And it was associated with our energy level, as was registered on the energy field picture. Compare my picture before and after visiting the Center: (Fig. 12, 13).

From the Buddhist Center we made our way to the Monroe Institute. It was only about 20 minutes drive, and for this time, sitting near Tenzin, we discussed his next visit to Russia and St. Petersburg.

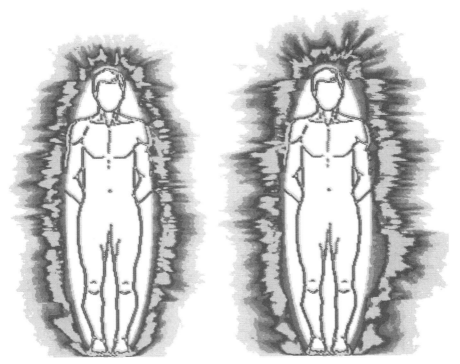

Fig.12. EPI image in the morning   *Fig.13. EPI image after visiting Buddhist Center*

In the beginning of the Twentieth century an outstanding Buddhist physician Peter Badmaev had founded a Buddhist temple in St. Petersburg. Badmaev had been a wonderful doctor and healer, applying all collection of Oriental medicine very effectively. He had come to St. Petersburg in the middle of 19th century with a small case of instruments and dried herbs and in some few years he had already got many clients, including even members of the tsar's court. This had given him an opportunity to build a large clinic in Saint Petersburg, and luxurious coaches had always been standing at its entrance, however in the days of free reception the poor had also crowded. The Buddhist temple, constructed with imperial permission in the nearest suburb of St. Petersburg, had become the center of attraction for the Buddhists from all North-West of Russia. The Bolsheviks had not been that tolerant as the monarchy, and so they had turned the praying people out of the temple, had made it a warehouse, but it had been so well constructed that even 70 years of desolation had not destroyed it. Now the temple is given back to the Buddhist community and in 15 minutes from the city center, near the beautiful park, one can enter the temple and listen to the plangent singing of the monks.

While we were talking with Tenzin we reached the Monroe Institute. Good parking. Beautiful complex of buildings. The Americans show good taste in building design, even using plywood. 90% of buildings in the USA are made of bars trimmed with plywood. Quick and cheap. Faced with stones or wood from the outside and looking quite presentable. But, in fact, such houses sway from the wind. And if a hurricane comes, it can easily take such a house and carry it to the unknown lands. As it was with the girl Dorothy in the tale "The Wizard of OZ" by Baum.

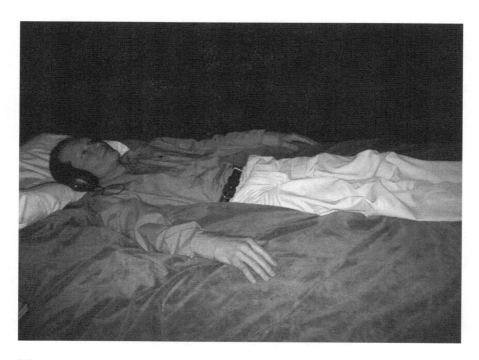

We were met and accompanied to the laboratory. Robert Monroe had been able to make his techniques widely well-known, introduce them to Pentagon and secret cervices, and receive recognition. For many years the Monroe Institute offers everybody a week course of personality transformation on the basis of special procedure. Training of this type was offered to Tenzin and me.

We took the initial pictures of fingertips. Then I was guided to a small room padded with black material inside. Practically all the room was occupied by a water bed, and when I lay on it, my body was suspended in a state of semi-weightlessness. Big earphones were put on my ears, the door was closed, and I found myself in total darkness. A thin melody sounded in the ears, and soon it filled all my being, all the space, breaking over the body as waves. The tune of the melody was changing from time to time, but it was not even a melody, it was the sound of waves, crackling of the silence, rustling of the darkness. Sound waves were pricking the body, stretching or pressing it, it was a peculiar sensation, although not the most interesting I had ever experienced in my life.

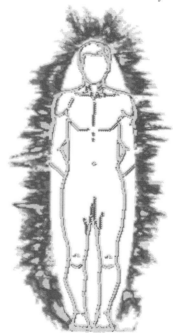

From time to time a soft voice inquired about my state, though there were no devices measuring the state. In about 10 minutes the session ended, and colleagues helped me to come out of the chamber. They certainly helped me because I was stoned and my head was swimming. That was clearly seen in the picture of my field: Nothing remained from the good state after the Buddhist Center (Fig. 14).

Fig. 14. EPI image after visiting Monroe Institute

This was the goal of the session, as explained by the staff of the Monroe Institute. Ultra low frequency sounds were applied through the ear⬜phones, and frequencies in right and left ears slightly differed. This caused desynchronization of the work of the right and left cerebral hemispheres. (Remember that we already discussed problems of the right and left brain). A human being left his usual stable state, and common perception of the world was violated. Many people suddenly understood that the outer world could be perceived otherwise, not just in its usual way, and this evoked the understanding that it was possible to live in different ways, and take everything which happens in one's life from different points of view. I heard from some Americans that a week course at the Monroe Institute helped them to fully change their attitude to life. To come out of the routine flow of life and problems and make the next step as a new person. Our life mainly depends not on the fact where we live, but how we think about it. Perhaps, the Monroe technique of the frequency influence might turn out to be useful for the psychological rehabilitation of veterans of war, refugees, people who survived hard psychological traumas. As well as for many people suffering from neurosis, heightened irritation, and inner dissatisfaction. To push from the usual platform, to break the routine circle, to get away from numbness, in order to then sit and think: what shall be done next?

I started doing analysis of the dynamic change of the field. (We took time dynamics from one finger within several seconds, and then carried out Fourier-analysis of spectrum). As a result, we obtained the curve (see Fig. 15) characterizing the main frequencies of the energy field. Based on this curve, the main frequencies were calculated. Computer calculations took a couple of minutes, and when I demonstrated the results, the Institute personnel started to examine the curves with special attention. Then one of them said:

"But these are the same frequencies we applied to your ear-phones. And this graph is the frequency curve which appears when two frequencies shifted relative to one another are superimposed. It took us two years of work to obtain such a graph from the analysis of encephalograms. And you did it in 5 minutes! Astonishing! How did you manage to do that?"

After that we were discussing for half an hour what all that would have meant and what we should do with this. Both parties were satisfied. They, because their ideas were proven, we, since we managed to do that. We said good-bye to each other in the best mood, although it hardly influenced the picture of my field: my head was swimming. I didn't know whether I was coming or going.

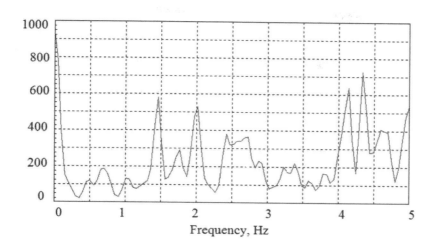

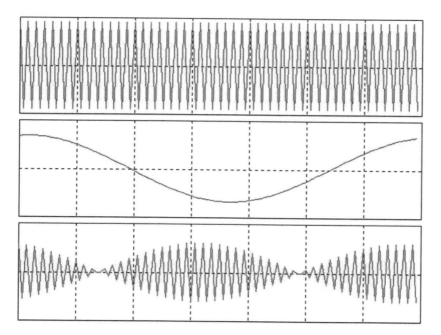

Fig. 15. Frequency dynamics of the Energy Field.
Main frequencies of the Energy Field.

Skeptic. Your examples with the change of energy field are not very convincing. All this is self-suggestion. They inculcated you with their ideas, and you fell under their influence.

Author. First of all, the result is important in many cases, even if we do not fully understand what is going on. If the head ache eases off from a finger flick, let us use this flick as a method of treatment. Then some day scientists will investigate the deep mechanisms. Of course, if there is somebody interested to investigate. Second, selfsuggestion is an important component of treatment. If you wish to be healthy- be healthy. Pessimists get ill more seriously and more often. And, finally, there are methods of objective estimation of state, and bioelectrography is a very sensitive method, but it is not so easy to affect me. So, if there is influence, you can not hide from it.

Skeptic. All your changes might be just variations. Measured now - one result, in an hour - absolutely another. Body temperature, for example, can show you a lot: 36,6°C - good, 37,2°C - bad. Your pictures are something different.

Author. Finally I heard a serious question from you. Your professional skill grows. I can give you quite a substantiated answer. A special research was performed with a group of ill and healthy people. They were measured with 1 hour and 1 day's interval. 80% of participants showed that the variability did not exceed 6-8%. For some people these numbers were higher, but only for the EPI-images taken without filter, i.e. for psychological field. Parameters remain invariable within many months for people with stable psyche and normal state of health. Deviations indicate coming diseases, potential problems. For instance, look at the EPI diagrams of state of one and the same person, measured in different points of time during one year: (Fig. 16) As we see, 8 curves quite exactly reproduce one another. This means that the state of the person remained very stable. And now pay attention to the curve in the center. That day the person poisoned himself with bad sausage, and his energy level had drastically fallen, particularly in the area of intestines. What was more, the measurement had been done before he felt the symptoms of poisoning.

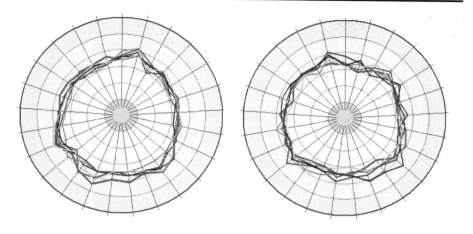

Fig.16. EPI diagrams of a person during the year

AFRICAN ZOMBIE AND WORLD TERRORISM

> *The Lord is my light and my*
> *salvation - whom shall I fear?*
> *Psalm 27:1 Of David*

For many years one of the main topics of our research has been the Altered States of Consciousness (ASC). What is this? Imagine that you live an ordinary life: you are occupied with everyday activity doing your job, meeting other people and thinking where to eat something tasty this night. If we ask you by the end of the day where you have been and what have you been doing you will more or less clearly describe your activity. But let us consider another situation: a scientist writes a treatise of his life, a student gets ready for the state exams, a youth in love imagines the eyes of his beloved girl. They are so preoccupied that they do not notice anything happening around. Another striking case: a sleep-walker who can walk along the roof ridge and never loose balance if nobody wakes him up. If somebody does, he will fall down. Here is the main obvious difference of the normal state of consciousness from the altered state: in the normal state an individual controls his surrounding, in the altered state one fully lives in his or her own inner world...

At midnight we gathered in a small glade, surrounded by a wall of tropical trees. South America, Peru, February, middle of the equatorial forest. We are sitting silently, waiting, strange presentiment as if something settled in the air. A priest with a drum appears, starts a slow rhythm. It reminds of something? Sure, it is modern rap, but slow. The second priest takes out a clay bottle in the form of a jaguar, pulls out the wooden plug, and pours a little bit of green liquid in a clay glass. He stretches it out to the closest one in the group: "Ready? Haven't changed your mind?" Hesitating for a second, the person takes the glass and drinks the liquid, and with evident relief lies on the mat. The priest holds out the glass to the next one. My turn comes. There is no way back, so I resolutely take the glass and drink it up. A grassy bitterish taste. No alcohol. Now we have to wait until it starts its action.

The course of this ceremony called Ajurvasco is very typical of such occasions. There should be a group of people, rhythmic music and some drug. Ajurvasco in Peru, Peyotl in Mexico, Cashassa in Brazil, medovuha (honey beverage) in ancient Russian ceremonies.

In half an hour the liquid begins to have its effect. The surrounding landscape distorts, tree branches take a winding shape, they move, as if alive, big villous stars are seen through them. I look around and suddenly see that the glade is full of snakes. They are everywhere: in the grass, under the snags, on tree branches. I am not fond of catching vipers and grass snakes, but this picture does not cause any unpleasant feelings: the snakes seem to be part of the environment and do not pose any threat. At the same time, looking around, I suddenly understand where the ancient art of the South American civilizations came from: it is obvious that ancient painters saw the world through the prism of Ajurvasco and Peyotl, and the surrounding in a phantasmagoric distorted form.

The green liquid was doing its bit: everything was boiling up inside and my body was more and more seized with weakness. I glanced around: my companions took most scenic poses: somebody was walking to and fro, squatting down, somebody was running, moving in a circle on all fours, and another one was roaring in fits of laughter. Suddenly my consciousness went blank and I felt I was a jaguar, a powerful cat, I felt strong legs, fangs, velvety fur all over the body, and a supple docile tail. I felt serene and powerful, my bulging eyes devoured the faintest movements in the foliage of the jungles, and my ears were moving slightly gathering all sounds of the night forest. This was a calm of a compressed spring, keeping its energy up to the final jump. A threat - the spring straightens up and the stored energy falls onto the victim in a terrible deadly blow.

That was not the only metamorphosis I experienced that night. The body was squirming in cramps of weakness and sickness, and the spirit traveled in the astral realm.

During the whole ceremony a few people watched the group. They cleaned the sweat from the wet bodies, drew aside and washed away the signs of deep physical cleanings; they knew no shame and no fastidiousness. Everything was natural in that illusive night world. And what was more they took EPI-grams of all the participants with portable equipment from time to time.

See the pictures. First one is the state of a human field before the beginning of the ceremony: (Fig. 17).

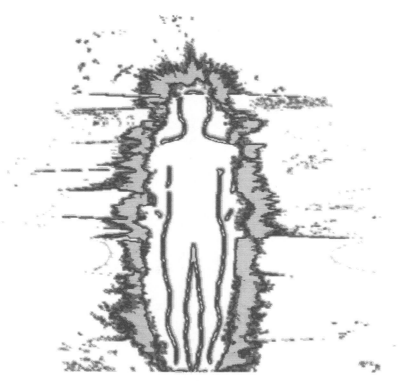

Fig.17. EPI image before the Ajurvasco ceremony

A powerful, strong field, physically and mentally active person. Now another picture, in the middle of the ceremony, when the poison started its destructive effect: (Fig. 18) As you see, the entire right part of the glow is practically missing and the left one is even brighter as compared with the initial state. But the right part corresponds to the left brain, pertaining to logic, speech, control of behavior. It becomes clear why the participants of the ceremony were laughing, crying, and crawling as children: they could not control their behavior. This is why they were dragged aside periodically. At the same time the left part - the right brain - is super-active. This is the source of emotions, imagination, feelings, and subconscious sensations. All those vivid images and visions came from there. By the end of the ceremony (Fig.

80

19) the right part of the glow gradually recovered, but this required several hours. Ancient Peruvian traditions say that by the end of the ceremony the field should be "closed", otherwise a person becomes affected by all outer influences and attacks.

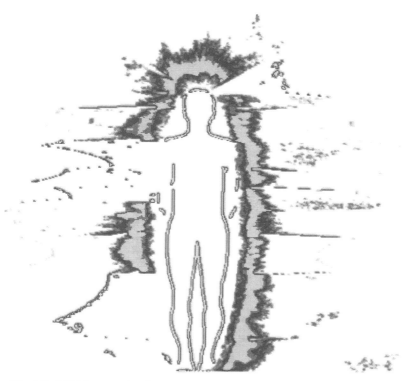

Fig.18. EPI image in the process of the Ajurvasco ceremony

81

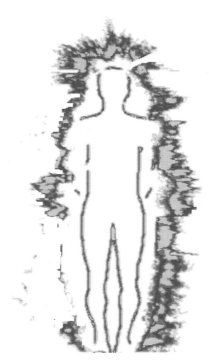

Fig.19. EPI image after the Ajurvasco ceremony

Our practical experience also brought us to an empirical conclusion that the "breaks" and "holes" in the field picture make the human field vulnerable to the physical and psychological influences. As if, indeed, foreign agents penetrate into the body through these beaks and do their destructive job. Which agents? Bacteria, viruses and protozoa on the physical level, bad thoughts on

Now look at the break in the head area. It is marked with an arrow in the picture. Isn't it like a channel? It remains after the end of the ceremony. Maybe this is really a channel connecting a person with another informational space? American science fiction films play up this topic very often; science makes only first uncertain assumptions.

Skeptik. So, why did you do this? Poison yourself with a strange potion to grow a tail! Go to the Zoo, stay in front of a cage - and imagine you are a beast! A waste of time again!

Author. Such a habit - to try all experiments myself. In order to adequately evaluate stories from people who were tested. And from the practical point of view all this has direct connection to our life. And, unfortunately, a tragic one. I will tell you another story.

In the Middle Ages a fortress rose in the Arabian mountains. The sheikh, tired of the feats of arms, secluded himself in his lost nook of this world. But the caravan leaders told dark stories about this mysterious fortress and preferred not to stay overnight in these mountains. And the dark stories weren't fairy tales.

The sheikh recruited most skillful and strong warriors from all countries, seducing them with lavish payment. The warriors were training in military art in the fortress and competed with one another. They were praying mornings and evenings, and skilled mullahs taught them surahs of the Koran. The warriors were forbidden to leave the fortress, but they were fed well and their wages were paid regularly. The only thing which was inconvenient for them was the absence of any women in the fortress. In a few weeks of such life the blood started boiling up and sparks of rage appeared in their eyes.

And then the sheikh invited a young warrior for a talk. He tenderly asked about his life, native land, and poured more foamy wine in the bowl. The youth did not notice how he fell asleep, but having opened his eyes he found himself in a beautiful marble hall with fountains and pools, where the blue water streamed and its drops sprinkled the meadows of bright live flowers. But brighter than all paints and more vivid than all the waterfalls were the young beautiful girls, surrounding the youth's bed. They were tender, caressing and accessible, it seemed that everything invented by Humanity in the art of passion and love was accumulated in this hall. Thus hours and days had passed, in passion and feasts, but suddenly, having awaken, the youth saw the known stone loopholes of the fortress, and the sheikh sitting in the same pose in front of him.

"Surprised?" the sheikh asked. "You've visited Paradise, my young friend, and met beautiful Gurias there. Weren't they gorgeous? I transferred you there with my magic, and a moment in this life seemed a week in that one. This entire castle is built with my magic. Do you want to serve me, so that I will show you the way to Paradise, or you will prefer a usual boring mode of living?"

Usually the youth agreed unhesitatingly, and those who didn't, did not live long. And the warrior was taught the art of hiding and killing, not with the weapon, but with any other improvised means: from pin to finger. And little by little a thought that if they die by the order of the sheikh they would go to this Paradise, to the Gurias, was put into the mind of all these warriors.

A few decades later the warriors of the mysterious castle, Assassins as they were called in the East, started playing a significant role in the policy of Arabic countries. The sheikh sent an ultimatum to the ruler of an area or country ending with the words: "If you don't carry out my requirements by the end of the big moon, you will die". The rulers threw away the paper with laughter and looked at the ranks of their faithful guardsmen, but at the proclaimed time a snake crawled out from the sleeve of a dervish and bit the ruler, or a visiting merchant, bowing, brought a Damascus saber to the ruler and plunged it immediately into his chest. The guards tore

Assassins in pieces on the spot, but they did not even resist as they were anticipating their meeting with the Gurias.

The mystic fortress intimidated the rulers of the East for centuries, until it was wiped off the face of the earth by the troops of Tamerlan, who destroyed both warriors and Gurias with a horse raid.

Doesn't this story remind you of something? Boeing airliner attacks on the New York skyscrapers, Palestinian boys blowing themselves up in the buses and discos of Israel, Japanese kamikaze storming American ships in "one-time" planes, Chechen terrorists taking hostages in a Moscow theater and Beslan school? A person means nothing to terrorists and rulers. Just a pawn in the play.

Skeptic. But how does this relate to the state of consciousness? The lads are paid well and proclaimed heroes ☐ so they are ready to give their lives.

Author. It's not so easy. I will promise ten thousand to your family if you jump from the tenth floor. Don't want to? That's it. Money is not the most significant thing in these situations, although it also plays its role. The most important is a special training of consciousness, which is transferred to a special state with a series of methods. Important elements: training is performed in a group, whose participants strengthen the intention of one another, rhythmic music is used, or rhythmic frequencies, tuning up one's brain and slogans are advanced, so that a person feels his uniqueness, peculiarity, and difference from all other groups. This is a special, highly professional training, based on strict selection and subtle knowledge of psychology and bioenergetics.

Evil forces use most secret mechanisms of human consciousness. They have perfected their devilish techniques and direct them against Humanity. American employees, Israeli students and Russian housewives turn out to be similarly unprotected against treacherous attacks of the kamikaze. When one's own life is not important, who will think about somebody else's life?

Skeptic. And what is the way out of this? What can we do to withstand this Evil attack?

Author. Only one way out ⬜ distribution of information and openness. The more open the society becomes, the more youths join the highest achievements of civilization, and the less the conditions to bring up kamikazes can be created. When a person sees perspectives in life, he doesn't want to say good-bye to it. When nothing good is in life, no regret comes about it. And, naturally, it's necessary to investigate consciousness, the powerful force which is capable of making great transformations and great evil.

THE SPIRIT HOVERED ABOVE THE WATERS...

The Light of Divine Amaterasu shines forever

Munetada

In November, 2001, I was invited to speak at the World Parapsychology Congress in Basel, Switzerland. The Congresses in Basel are held every year, already for 20 years, and gather several thousands of people from Europe and all over the world. Each year they are dedicated to different topics related to strange phenomena; this time the topic was healing. We will discuss this question in more details some day, now I would like to describe just one direction of research which was started at this congress and has become wide spread.

Basel is a nice small town near the French border. Even the airport is in France, and a special corridor leads you from the arrival hall to Switzerland. The old city was constructed in the Fourteenth through Sixteenth centuries, and taking a walk along the narrow streets, you feel a real spirit of the Medieval Europe. Crossing the bridge you find yourself in a modern standard city where one of the points of interest is the Congress Hall. A big six-store building, a five-star hotel in one part and forum in the other with several big halls, a great two-level foyer and a presentation floor. A part of the World Parapsychology Congress is an exhibition. Hundreds of companies and individuals offer magic crystals, charged amulets, Indian, American Indian, Shaman objects, oils, aromas, food supplements, books, and cassettes. The Medieval inquisition would have burned all these objects as the means of witchcraft, together with the sellers. Now this is no longer the rule, and if something is burned in the squares now, say, bad books of bad authors, this is a means of advertising campaign done in order to increase the sales. Most important in the modern world is to attract attention to oneself; the means is secondary.

Healers work right there in special cabins, our Moscovite Alexey Nikitin among them. Many years ago at a conference in Sochi he got acquainted with a Swiss married couple, and there at the conference, he cured the husband who had an acute radiculitis attack. They invited Alexey to visit them and asked him to give treatment to their relative. The effect turned out to be so strong that from then on Alexey spent several months a year in Switzerland, healing people and giving lectures on healthy life-style. In spite of his being overweight Alexey rushes about in the hall continuously exchanging bows with friends and broadly smiling to all the others. Cordial smiles are an obligatory attribute of life in Switzerland.

The Congress opens at 10 a.m. and does not calm down until 10 p.m. This is first of all the place of meetings and acquaintances. People from all over the world come here; it's a unique opportunity to speak with one another. After my lecture in the central hall and a three-hour presentation in a small hall accommodating 250 places, people from different countries one after another approached our table in the foyer. There were quite interesting individuals among them. The director of a big biological institute in Germany, a political figure from Chile, the head of a clinic in Italy. Once Alexey introduced a lively man about 60 years old with penetrating black eye,

"Konstantin, pay attention to this gentleman. This is a famous German healer Christos Drossinakis."

The famous German healer was Greek with a typical Mediterranean appearance, quick speech, and lively tenacious look. As soon as we met he offered to organize joint experiments with the mass-media and TV people. "Without publicity there are no prosperity", says a Zulu folk proverb. In a few minutes we were surrounded by a crowd of spectators and TV reporters. Christos brought a middle-aged gentleman, and we measured his energy field: (Fig. 20).

Then Christos stood behind his back, his expression became serious, even dark, a standard smile disappeared, and he started to move his hands at the distance from the patient's back. The session ended in five minutes, and we measured the fingers again. The effect was obvious even for not well-informed person (Fig. 21)

The public applauded; with a contented look, Christos began to give an interview.

For the next step we measured his field in the initial state and in the process of healing. The initial field (Fig. 22) was all distorted and not uniform, which, however, corresponded to the overexcited state of Drossinakis during the congress. I had strong doubts that we would be able to find something interesting. Then Christos came into a special state and we took each finger in the moment of maximum activity at his command. A few seconds of computer processing, and an image which considerably differed from those of all the usual people appeared on the screen (Fig. 23).

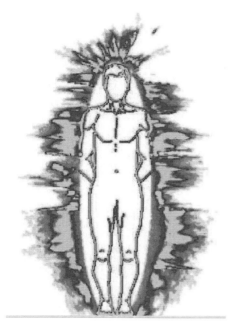 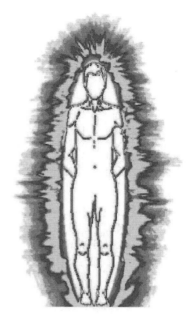

Fig.20. Initial EPI image of a
person

Fig.21. EPI image of a person
after healing

This was not a common case in our practice. Indeed, as strong as an ox at any rate judging by his energy. We repeated experiments several times during the congress, and every time the result was interesting. At the closing ceremony I demonstrated the data obtained with Drossinakis, and he was smiling with pleasure and shaking hands with all acquaintances. We said good-bye as friends, and Christos promised to come to St. Petersburg in order to hold a detailed experiment. I did not pay much attention to this: what don't people promise in the moments of excitation!

But that time I was wrong. In February 2002 we were holding a workshop on EPI bioelectrography for foreign colleagues, and Drossinakis turned out to be one of the participants. The idea was that during the workshop we would organize a number of experiments.

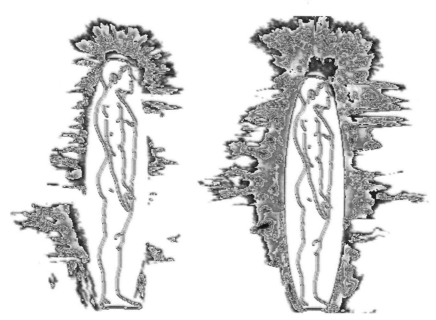

Fig.22. Initial EPI image of Drossinakis   *Fig.23. EPI image of Drossinakis in the process of healing*

A very interesting and lively company gathered at the workshop: researchers from the USA, Germany, Ireland, Sweden, Switzerland, England, Israel, and India. The well-known to the reader Robert Van de Castle was among the participants. He told that before the departure he had made a cardiogram, and the doctors had strongly advised him not to travel anywhere.

"Considering you are 76 years and have a bad cardiogram, you need to go to hospital, instead of Russia. Otherwise we can expect the worst. However Bob was a fatalist and an optimist. Therefore, he invested in a good insurance and flew to St. Petersburg, although he did not look very good."

In the mornings we gathered in the computer classroom, to study the mysteries of EPI bioelectrography. In the evenings we went to the philharmonic hall or theater we wished that the guests should get an idea about our culture. One of the days we went for a walk to the suburb parks of Pushkin. The walk was announced as "Trip to the Russian Winter Forest", and the reality justified its name. It was -25°C (13°F) that day. The sun peeped out, the trees covered with snow were sparkling in the sun. A short walk in the park came out to be enough: the frozen Europeans, Americans and Indians were happy to enter the warm hall of a local restaurant. There they got the idea of taking a glass of vodka as they had returned from the frost! The first glass was followed by the second, then the third one, after which it was found that the Indians, Americans and Europeans were not that bad in Russian folk dances. In the heat of all this revelry I glanced at Robert and saw that he was not looking well: he turned pale and held on to the heart. I approached Drossinakis and asked him, "Christos, let us start the process of healing right now."

He agreed straightaway, took Robert aside, offered him a seat, and started making his passes. In half an hour having gained color Bob joined the whole group. In the next days Drossinakis repeated sessions regularly, and, of course, we took EPI- grams. Every day the picture became better and better, and Bob joked more and more often and cheerfully. A natural shortcoming of Drossinakis' sessions was that after his influence the skin had red spots.

By the way, I observed such an effect with several other powerful healers. But the biggest impression was when one of them, correcting my aching back, asked,

"Do you mind if I burn your skin slightly?"

"How?"

"I will increase the energy for a deeper penetration into the tissues, but the skin usually burns out at that."

"OK, I like to test everything new on myself".

The healer continued his passes, and I felt light warmth in the back, but when I looked in the mirror later I found a second-degree burn 5 x 7 cm in size. It was closing up for about two weeks, but radiculitis did not show its effect for about two weeks after that.

After coming back to the USA, Robert went to the doctor. The latter made a cardiogram and was amazed,

"Strange. Your cardiogram is like that of a twenty-year old guy. I have observed you for a long time and have never seen such good data."

By the way, before the departure Robert Van de Castle approached me and said,

"Konstantin, I want to share one of my dreams with you. Remember Justine told her dream when I was calling her? Remember that I mentioned some device in her dream? Well, I saw that device in a dream many years ago. I clearly saw how I was using it in my experiments. And do you know what that device was? What did it measure? Right! It measured energy field of a human being! And now we start a joint program with you! Well, isn't it great? How can one remain being a materialist after such a phenomenon?

I had totally agreed with him. I have seen so many things during the long years of work that it would be enough for another hundred of similar tales. But I still don't stop wondering. Otherwise it gets boring.

In the next series of experiments we examined the influence of energy on water. We developed a technique of measuring the induced glow of water, and measured many interesting effects. Water is a magic liquid, the basis of life, it easily takes up information, stores and transfers it. In order to be useful for life - live water, it is hardly sufficient to let it pass through a filter, although this is better than nothing. But this is a separate topic, and we will come back to it. In our winter workshop we were interested in the change of fluorescence of water under the influence of human energy state.

We connected the measuring device to the instrument and began measurement. Drossinakis was sitting near the instrument fixing his stare at the device. In about one minute he said,

"Ready. You can measure it."

We checked the measurement. Indeed, the amplitude of the glow of the liquid sample changed: (Fig. 24).

I wasn't surprised as I expected such a result. And we had done similar experiments with Alan Chumak, Albert Ignatenko, Alexey Nikitin, Victor Philippi, and other skilled native craftsmen. We had even developed a technique of testing intuitive capabilities on this basis. So, I was interested not in the fact of influence, but how big it was. Drossinakis demonstrated quite a strong effect.

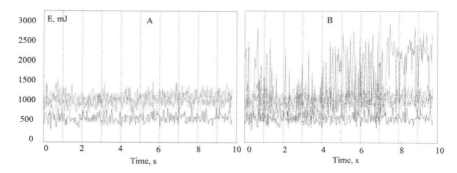

*Fig.24. Change of the amplitude of the glow of the liquid sample
(A - initial; B - after)*

The foreign participants were highly impressed with the experiment. For the first time they saw how it was possible to visually demonstrate the influence of a human being on the material world. As water is the basis of any biological system, from an ameba to a human; if you are able to influence the water you can influence anything.

Of course, we repeated the experiment. With a positive result. Naturally, several guests tried to repeat sessions. With no result. No one then had any doubts on the effectiveness of Christos' influence. That fact gave a cause for a few toasts at the gala dinner.

In spring I happened to go to Germany for business, where I was to visit Munich, Dresden, Frankfurt, and fly back from Dusseldorf. In order to freely move, I rented a car. It is a special pleasure to travel in Germany by car, as there are no speed limitations on the highways and it's possible to drive as fast as the car goes. My "Renault" was able to speed up to 190 km/h (110 mph). Only once I could make 210 km/h (130 mph) downhill. You can drive and not be afraid that a local policeman appears from behind the turn.

In Frankfurt I stopped at Drossinakis' small apartment filled with antique furniture. It turned out that in his spare time Drossinakis restored antique furniture, which he gathered at the stores in Greece, Czechia, and France. Christos organized meetings with scientists, journalists; a big article was prepared based on the results of our experiments. While drinking sweet Greek wine he suggested an idea,

"Look, Konstantin, I'm going to Japan for demonstrations in a month. Why don't we influence water from Japan?"

"Great idea, Christos!" I exclaimed, pouring wine into the glass. "We can also influence wine".

"In Russia good wine is expensive, and there's no sense to work with bad one. Come to Greece, I will show you good wine!"

"I'll take you at your word! I will certainly come some day. I have always dreamt to swim in the Aegean Sea. And it's not a bad idea to influence water from Japan."

No sooner said than done. On the agreed day we put 5 similar bottles with drinking water on the window in the laboratory in St. Petersburg. Each had a colored sticker: red, blue, green, etc. At some moment unknown to us, from 12 a.m. to 1 p.m. Drossinakis should have influenced two bottles from Japan, leaving the rest untouched. At 1 p.m. we took samples from all the bottles and made measurements. Naturally, before the experiments, in the morning the samples from all bottles had been taken, which had demonstrated that the water had been the same in all bottles.

Look at the results of measurements. (Fig. 25).

Each curve represents the dynamics of change of the water drop's glow with the course of time, during 10 seconds. As you see, the three upper curves are rather smooth, and the two lower ones demonstrate quite restless behavior: first the glow increases, then decreases, which is typical of active, live water. It is obvious that the character of these two samples differs from all the others. And this can be connected with the mental influence of Drossinakis. The only discrepancy, as it became clear afterwards, was that he had been tried to influence the blue and red bottles, and we observed changes in the green and the red ones.

We repeated the experiment from Japan once again, and twice from Germany. The effect was observed in all cases (Fig. 26).

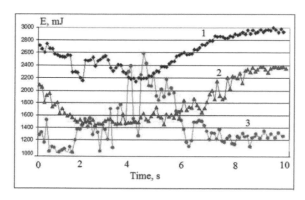

Fig.25. Time dynamics of change of the water drop's glow. 1,2 – typical signal; 3 – water under the mental influence

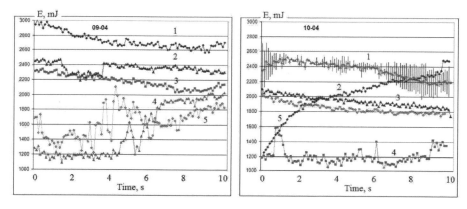

Fig.26. Time dynamics of change of the water drop's glow in different days, 1,2,3 – typical signal; 4,5 – water under the mental influence

Skeptic. Pack it in! These were random variations. Something got into the bottle. Or somebody grabbed it with dirty hands.

Author. These are the factors which are easily controlled. The staff of a laboratory with good reputation will first of all verify the reproducibility and repeatability of results.

Skeptic. And what happens with your "charged" water then? For how long does it keep the signs of influence?

Author. According to our data, for about 24 hours. It is being transformed, at that. As we have seen, the primary chaotic oscillations were changed with a certain regular curve, which was reproduced within 24 hours. But the character of this curve was still different from that of the initial waters. So, some processes did took place in water.

Skeptic. And what processes?

Author. Well, this is a topic of a special discussion. Some other day, now it's time to go and drink tea.

Skeptic. Wait, wait a little. Are you saying that it is possible to just that easily influence the surrounding world with the consciousness?

Author. Well, not that easily, one needs talent and training in order to do that, but the fact exists. All experiments discussed in this chapter indicate that human consciousness can influence physical processes of our world.

Skeptic. And maybe all this is your imagination, experimental errors?

Author. Our results were reproduced in other countries; several laboratories in the world are doing such research, so it is already obvious that these are not experimental errors and not imagination.

Skeptic. This way you will talk to the point that a thought can move mountains, and prayer can raise the dead.

Author. The dead are a special topic, but the influence of prayer is quite measurable. My following story will tell you about that.

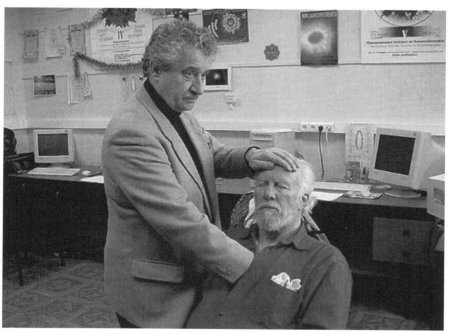

CAN A PRAYER BE MEASURED?

Following the light,
The sage takes care of all
Lao Tzu, 6th century BC

Once a couple of years ago a nice middle-aged woman approached me at a workshop in Chicago.

"My name is Janet Dunlop. Professor, may I discuss my scientific project with you?" she asked timidly.

"Of course, let us go and sit somewhere and discuss your project", I replied willingly. Several dissertations with the application of our methods and approaches have been done in the USA. Each dissertation is serious research, requiring a few years of painstaking work, and positive results always raise scientific authority of both the author of the dissertation and the methods developed in it.

But when I heard the idea of Janet's work, my first desire was to dissuade her from this. A chance to receive some results seemed to be too improbable. But this elegant, delicate lady turned out to be uncommonly persistent. It seemed that she had been developing this idea for a long time and decided to put it into practice, notwithstanding all difficulties.

Within the two next years Janet attended all my workshops in the USA and Canada. It was astonishing how this lady with an absolutely humanitarian spirit, had made up her mind to master the computer, starting from scratch, and moreover, to use it for a serious scientific work. Dozens of people helped her: one taught her to work with equipment; another one made mathematic calculations, the third one selected data from literature. As a result, Janet made her dissertation, defended it in the University, and demonstrated her level before all the Skeptics.

Indeed, "...when a person wants something very much, the Universe does everything to help". This is from the "Alchemist" by an Argentinean writer Paulo Coelho.

What is the essence of Janet's work? She lives in Missouri - an American remote place. Blocks of nice cottages separated from one another by flower gardens and playgrounds. Each cottage is occupied by one family, and everything on credit - this is more convenient from the viewpoint of paying taxes, even if the family has money. They go to a supermarket once a week; if you forgot something you have to drive another 40 minutes to the closest store or gas station. There are no stalls with beverages there. And all shops close at 7 p.m. If you did not come in time means you came late. People drive to work for one hour or one hour and a half. Every day. As a rule, in the mornings there are traffic jams in one direction, and in the evening - in another. Those who can work at home feel much better; therefore computer home work with Internet data exchange becomes more and more popular in the USA. What is more, there is no necessity to see the boss every day. In short, American remote places are inhabited with solid people who make their life, having little in common with the noisy gangs and parties of big megapolises.

And in such a remote place, Janet gathered 85 men - volunteers in the age of 35- 60 years. Men □ in order not to depend on the variability of female hormonal background during several months of experiment. The most active age, although the youthful jumps and fluctuations have already ended. In addition, the men selected should not have had acute or chronic diseases, as well as bad habits like alcoholism and drug addiction. I doubt that it would have been possible to gather such a group in Russia. Moreover, to persuade them to take part in the experiments without a glass of spirits. Conditions of Janet's experiment would have been broken right away.

The state of all volunteers was measured before the beginning of experiments: psychological tests, blood analysis, physiological indices, and parameters of glow of fingers. After that all volunteers were randomly divided into two groups. Nobody of them knew which group he pertained to. And they continued living their usual life: went to work, played with children, and visited church on Sundays. The only difference was that each of the members of one group was prayed for in the mornings and evenings, during a whole month.

The topic is not new for Western science. Relation between science and religion, materialism and spirituality has been a subject of active discussions for more than a century. Elena Blavatskaya from Russia, a genius dilettante, the founder of the theosophical movement, was one of the first who raised this question.

In the end of the Twentieth century this topic changed from a subject of theoretical discussion to an object of scientific experimental research. And the first aim which arose for many believing scientists was to prove that the belief, and particularly the prayer, exerted positive influence on the human state. Indeed, if God helps the believers, he has to give them good health first of all. Not for nothing are there so many stories about the longevity and health of monks. But there this can be explained by the influence of tranquil monastic life. And what about common people, believers and non-believers? Is there any statistical difference in the state of health?

Several large-scale sociological and epidemiological surveys were performed. In one of the most significant surveys, elderly people who had cardiac infarction were investigated for several years. They clearly demonstrated the criterion of their state of health, absolute survivability. All possible factors were taken into account: social status, standard of life, taking medicines, religiousness, etc. It turned out that the level of prosperity and comfort had not influenced the state of health. (The research was carried out in the USA, so there were no starving people among the investigated, but even in the USA the difference in the level of life of various groups of population is quite significant). Religiousness appeared to be an important factor: the believers lived statistically longer. But the most significant factor which surpassed all the others was quite unexpected for the researchers. This was the presence of a home friend, a cat or dog: people who had pets lived longer and were healthier. That's how it's important to have a pet nearby.

In other research, 800 patients were randomly selected in one of the biggest American hospitals, and a group of nuns was praying for their health every day. In a month the progress of treatment of these patients as compared to the control group of people who had practically the same diseases was analyzed. But the control group was not prayed for. The convalescence was statistically shorter in the group which had been prayed for, with all other factors remaining the same.

Such research requires large groups of tested individuals: several hundreds, or even thousands. For some the process goes up, for others - down, but everything is statistically averaged in the group. Classical statistics fully proves itself in such experiments!

In Janet's experiments the calculation was based on detecting subtle individual changes. The methods applied were to follow these changes on all the levels: physical, psychological, and field levels.

When the experiment was being planned I was trying to convince Janet to select people with at least some problems: physical or psychological. Then there would be a way to change for the better. But the persistent delicate lady held her own: she did not want any additional factors to influence the result.

In a month the measurements were repeated, and after processing it was found that no parameters changed. People were healthy and remained the same. This was the first conclusion from the statistics, performed for the whole group of 40 people in comparison with the control 40 persons (within the month 5 people were winnowed out because of different reasons). This was a great frustration for Janet. All her hard labor, sleepless nights at the computer, and long days in the library went to rack and ruin. But the mathematicians decided to stand back and began the analysis on the individual level, the level of each particular person. And such an approach was successful! What an insidious thing is that statistics!

It was discovered that 9 people from the experimental group (prayed for) differed from all the others by a complex of EPI parameters. I.e. those 9 people really changed during that month, while the state of all the others remained practically unchanged!

Skeptic. So where are the proofs that these changes took place as the result of prayer, and not some other factors, say flu or a jackpot.

Author. Of course, the experiment enabled us to disclose only the presence of changes, as compared to the control group. And, in principle, these changes could be caused by various factors, but Janet tried to consider these issues. Her questionnaire had special questions about diseases and important events. 5 people who had such events were eliminated from the study. Therefore, we hope that it was the prayer which was the significant factor causing the changes.

Skeptic. Haven't you tried to measure the influence of prayer directly?

Author. Several times, in different countries. It is especially vivid when the picture is taken before and after the prayer. Sincere believers demonstrate changes practically always. But the value of such experiments is considerably lower than the value of Janet's study. An individual prays consciously, his psyche and emotions are involved in this process, and he believes in the result. It's impossible to say whether the changes take place because of emotions or prayer. Although both exert positive influence on the state of health.

Skeptic. If everything were like that, the believers would live longer and wouldn't be ill! But there are a lot of them in the hospitals, not less than atheists!

Author. A lot of different factors influence us in our life. Both at physical and spiritual levels. Every minute we take in thousands of bacteria, consume kilograms of nitrates and nitrites, liters of spoiled water, we are exposed to bad thoughts and evil glances. Permanent war of the Good with the Evil goes on. Angels of light always protect their wards from attacks, but the latter themselves trustingly strive after the colored toys of the Kingdom of Evil. And how difficult it is to distinguish a God's messenger from the spirit-tempter! The tempter's speeches are sweet when he lures another victim into his net.

This is why there are so few people living a truly saintly life in an ecologically clean environment. Perhaps, monks on the Solovki or the Valaam Islands in the Far North of Russia or Tibetan monks. But in our life the main condition for health is an optimistic relation to life, correct nutrition, and prayer. If you believe in all this, it works. Well, as you see, now it can be measured.

CAN LOVE BE MEASURED?

The radiance of Buddha shines ceaselessly

Dhammapada

Recently we celebrated the fifty year birthday anniversary of one of our student friends. We drank to him, to his parents, to health, and then he stood up and raised his glass to his wife, with whom he has spent twenty years together and without whom his life would not be so rich and successful as it is. The guests supported the toast with pleasure, drank, and then one of the inveterate single men noticed,

"This is not love, this is a habit".

"It is not true, a habit is to clean the teeth in the morning, when you feel yourself uncomfortable without this, and love is when you can not be without each other for a long time", Andrey, the hero of the event objected.

"There are different stages of love: love to parents, love to homeland, love to children, love to three oranges", Boris entered into conversation.

"Real love is determined by what you are ready to sacrifice for your beloved woman", Andrey commented. He had always had an ability to formulate his thoughts briefly, but precisely.

"But is there a difference between the love for children and love for a sexual partner, although in both cases you are ready to sacrifice everything for their sake, even life," asked Ninochka, taking an elegant sip from a crystal liqueur-glass.

"Love has many sides", Valentin replied, "As the Indians say, 'Attraction of bodies gives birth to passion, Attraction of minds gives birth to respect, Attraction of souls gives birth to friendship. Unification of these three attractions gives birth to Love."

"But love can exist even if these three components are not equal to one another, or when they are different in size, "Shura said. "And love is paradoxical in its essence. We love not for something, but regardless something. That's the nature of loving people, when they don't notice the demerits of the object of their passion they build some ideal image in their soul, which often doesn't comply with reality."

"But the state of love, being in love completely changes the person, this is visible for all people around; he radiates something special into space", Lubasha exclaimed.

"And can love be measured?" Borya asked.

And at that point I recalled the experiments presented at the international conference in Lubljana, Slovenia, by the family of Starchenko.

It was a very pleasant trip. Together with Prof. Voeikov from the Moscow University we were invited to this conference by the University of Lubljana. Prof. Igor Kononenko, the organizer of the event, a mathematician, is one of the European leaders in the field of artificial intelligence. The field of his spiritual interest is consciousness, and its influence upon the surrounding world. As many other serious international scientists, he tries to scientifically substantiate the idea that our life is determined not only by material circumstances, but also by spiritual mood. He had carried out many experiments and finally had settled on our EPI Camera, as a device able to objectively register the influence of emotions and passionate fire upon the human state. Prof. Kononenko had measured the effect of meditation, prayer, Oriental physical and spiritual practices and had statistically proved their objective influence.

Slovenia is a small country situated between Italy, Austria, Hungary, and Croatia. The population is less than 2 million people there, and the whole country can be crossed all over by car in 4 hours. But this small territory has so many beautiful places that it is enough for a month's journey. Crystal mountain lakes with waterfalls and unassailable medieval castles, one of the largest caves in the world with stalactites and stalagmites, gorgeously beautiful underground lakes, and bare blind fish, living in total darkness. A castle standing on the edge above this cave had never been conquered. Once in the Middle Ages the attackers had been standing at its walls for a month and then had met the besieged in the nearby village - they had been cheerfully drinking beer. They had gone down into the cave through the secret passage and had come up through the underground labyrinths on the other side of the mountain. Small villages with durable stone houses, wooden barrels of wine in the cellars, unique for each territory and each vineyard. And the inhabitants consider it an honor if you come to them to drink a glass of wine with house cheese.

An astonishing concentration of talented people in this tiny country. Suffice it to say that the number of our EPI instruments per head there is bigger than in any other country of the world. Several laboratories working in the field of bioenergetics and obtaining interesting results are situated solely in Lubljana. We did not want to miss any presentation at the conference, which happens quite seldom at scientific meetings. But even at the generally high level, the presentation of the Anufrievs from Ekaterinburg attracted everybody's attention.

We had known this couple for a long time. The thin and elegant Elena - a consultant in psychology, living in emotions and intuition, and her husband Victor - a solid businessman, highly spiritual, a reliable and sincere person. They had organized a bioenergetic laboratory in Ekaterinburg, and owing to Victor's business grip and enthusiasm of Elena, this laboratory had become well-known in Ural, and their work had obtained recognition in the world. But let us give the floor to them.

"The aim of the present research is to study the effect of thoughts as the highest manifestation of human psychological activity, on human the psyche. The research was performed with the help of EPI Camera instrument developed by Prof. K. Korotkov, St. Petersburg, Russia. The instrument registers the pictures of EPI fluorescence of fingers which are further processed in computer and a spatial energy field is built around the human body. The capabilities of this instrument enabled us to visually see the changes taking place in the human energy field under the influence of various thoughts.

Research was done on practically healthy people during 2 years. The quantity of tested people: 50. Particularly interesting were the results obtained on close people with quite harmonized energy fields.

Previous research had been carried out by means of a cardiologic diagnostic complex using methods of mathematical analysis of heart rhythm variability (HRV), and it had been found that the thought and heart had been interconnected. The thought, as energy, could have measured the heart rhythm: decrease and increase the frequency of heartbeats, change vegetative balance in the regulation of cardiac activity and influence functional state of regulatory systems of the organism.

A thought of love, coming from one heart to the other in the form of a separate energy cluster, was fixed for the first time in the present research using Gas Discharge Visualization (EPI) technique. At present many scientists acknowledge that the thought has material nature, that the thought is energy. And this energy is everpenetrating. Numerous telepathic experiments have proven that neither the thickest wall nor long distance has been an obstacle for the thought. From 1919 to 1920's a well-known Russian scientist, doctor-psychologist and academician V.M. Bekhterev had performed a number of experiments on the directed transfer of thought to some distance. First the experiments had been performed on animals, and then on people. He proved scientifically that a person could mentally influence another one. In the 1920's a famous Indian biologist G. Boshe investigated the effect of human thought on vital activity of plants. In the 1930's and 1940's in the West many scientists had been researching the influence of thought and had made experiments on thought transfer (Adrian and Metius, England; Rein and MacDougall, USA; Brunler, Germany). A doctor⎕psychiatrist from California, Anita Mjul, had demonstrated that thoughts of different quality influence an individual in a different way, changing pulse frequency.

Modern scientific ideas about the world tell about the energy nature of all the living. And the basis of the Energy paradigm is the law of conserving energy. As soon as radioactivity had been discovered, it became obvious that matter is transferred into energy, although gradually. And Einstein's equation $E = mc^2$ gives grounds to speak not only on the transformation of matter into energy, but also on the reverse process ⎕ transformation of energy into matter, i.e. proves that energy and matter are a one in-two manifestation of one and the same universal substance.

The World paradigm of the ancients had always kept the notion about the single moving force of the Universe and the interconnection of all the living in the Cosmos. Different nations in different centuries had called this ever-basic cosmic energy in different ways: Qi in Ancient China, Prana and Vital force in Ancient India. Psychic energy in modern science. "The world process is the manifestation of the single world energy", considered V.M. Behterev, "and wherever the latter was found and in whatever forms, it is manifested everywhere in one and the same correlations and is subject to the same rules and laws". And "this sole world energy is transformed into nervous-psychological energy" in the human being. Thought as the highest manifestation of human psychic activity is also the highest demonstration of psychic energy.

We captured the emanation of psychic energy, coming not from the brains, but from the hearts of individuals while they were sending thoughts of love and good will through space and concentrating on a close, beloved person.

Fig. 27 represents the human energy field when thought "May the World feel the good" is sent into the space. Activation of heart energy center (heart chakra) takes place. The human energy field picture clearly demonstrates the emanation of energy from the heart, exceeding the width of the general energy field by two or three times, and a mass of emanation from the left little finger is observed on the EPI-grams of fingers. The energy field itself, on the whole, remains even, without breaks, holes, and without emanation from the other energy centers. The energy of love "flies" from the heart. The pulse increases by 10-15 beats a minute, at that.

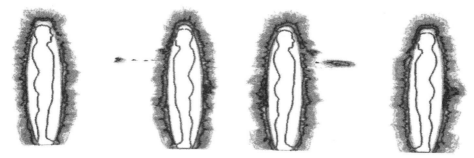

Fig.27. Exchange of Love between people

We managed to capture an energetically isolated cluster coming from the heart of the thought's sender to the heart of the thought's receiver when a significant level of concentration and sincerity was reached during the process of sending thought to the beloved person. On the EPI-grams of fingers, the thought that is sent is located in the heart sector of the left little finger, while the thought received is located in the heart sector of the right little finger.

We can distinguish the characteristics of the thought being sent. First, a clear image of the energy cluster, separated from the main energy field, appears. Secondly, the color and form of this cluster is very similar to that of the main field According to the level of brightness, the core of the cluster corresponds to the brightest part of the main aura of the finger or even exceeds it. The cluster may appear at different points of the heart sector and at different distances from the glow of the little finger.

We found the exact moment when the energy cluster of the thought that was sent appeared. The cluster was registered within 1-2 sec, regardless of the distance between the objects (experiments were performed both at 100 inches distance between participants and at 932 miles distance from one city to the other).

Many well-known scientists are preoccupied with the question where the thought is born. The Nobel Price laureate G. Eckles assumed that the brain is the acceptor of thought, and not the producer, i.e. it just accepts and processes thoughts and doesn't produce them itself. Academician N. P. Behtereva considers that this is not absolutely true. The brain does quite well with the simplest thoughts, but when the question is concepts, etc., it is really more complicated. In 1995 a professor of Melbourne University doctor Herst had made a discovery: he declared that the heart had been able to think independently, i.e. to change its rhythm irrespective of the brain. The results obtained with the EPI camera instrument prove this viewpoint. The thought felt deeply by the heart is born in the heart, is transferred by the heart, and is received by the heart. And the more heart feelings an individual puts in, i.e. sincerity into the transfer, the more obvious is the increase of pulse. Required heart energy is quasi attached to the thought, so that it has vital activity. In the Studies of Live Ethics, which came through Nicholas and Helena Roerichs it is said, "It is not the brain substance that thinks. Time has come for all to recognize that thought is born in the fire centers. Thought exists as something weighty and invisible, but it is necessary to understand that matter is not the only thing that matters. The thought is sent through the heart and is received through the heart, as well". Thus, for the first time, we registered the thought of love, coming from one heart to another one. Human thought is energy, which can influence plants, animals and the human being, that is, all the environment. In accordance with the law of energy conservation, the thought is indestructible. Mankind is constantly thinking in the process of its activity, making its contribution to the energetic of earth. And this means that each person should realize high responsibility for the quality of his or her thoughts.

Isn't it a wonderful research! Moreover, it's worth mentioning that the phenomenon of sending "love energy" has been registered many times, with different people, sincerely loving each other and sending their tender feelings to one another. So, it turns out that Love is really the only force that can withstand Evil and save Humanity from the coming catastrophes.

"GOD MODULE" OR A LIVING MACHINE?

The man has learnt from the machine to think
With dignity and talk with reason, too.
The man was shown that the Spirit's nothing
Compared to the matter, which is all;
The man himself is but an automaton,
The starry Cosmos is a clock-work; the Idea
Is but a product of the brain digestion.

Maximilian Voloshin, (1877-1932)
Russian poet and painter

Let us consider only some issues (however the most radical): What is Consciousness from the viewpoint of physics? What are its main features and qualities? What is life?

These questions have always been urgent issues for mankind; however they were the prerogative of philosophy. Exact sciences never tried to broach the subject. The concept of 'consciousness" in modern science does not exist. Such situation has arisen since the days of Rene Descartes who justified the division of material and spiritual. The material is studied by science, the spiritual is the sphere of religion, and these areas do not overlap. The brain is part of the software of our lives, and the body is the executive mechanism. This approach enabled to get rid of the church pressure and ensure the free development of scientific thought in XVIII-XIX centuries. But the same approach in the past XX century became an obstacle for the development of the sciences on consciousness. In the academic science the official point of view was accepted that consciousness was a product of brain activity, just as bile is a product of the liver. Later the notion triumphed that nothing except the cells exists in the biological basis of life. This concept was announced as the foundation of biology.

Naturally, numerous concepts were proposed supporting the notion of consciousness: from total denial of mental events, called behaviorism, to idealism, which negates the physical world and considers all events as a mental constructions. Between these

110

extremes there is a psychophysical parallelism, connecting mental events exclusively with processes in the brain, the functionalism making the analogy between mental events and computer programs, the panpsychism attributing to everything a form of consciousness, etc.

In recent decades, the scientific world has increased interest in scientific substantiation of the relations of matter, mind and spirit. Formerly, a serious scholar would lose reputation if he started to argue on this topic. Now this topic within a more limited range is becoming a subject of studies included in the processes of consciousness, and even such scholars as a Nobel laureate F. Crick[2] get involved with it. How do we perceive the world and ourselves in it, is the brain the source of consciousness only just an executive mechanism, where does the religious perception arise? These and similar questions are the subject of serious research and debates. And if the professional scientists are taking up some business, they do it thoroughly and with great consideration. I had the opportunity to attend several scientific symposia on the subject, and each time among ordinary general arguments there were some serious, carefully conducted studies. Revolutionary results were obtained using computed tomography of the brain. This is the area using the most modern multi-million dollar equipment for monitoring neurophysiological processes in real time.

The latest series of experiments is related to the study of the processes of religious perceptions and religious ecstasy.

Merechanur Ramachantran from the Center of Consciousness and Brain of the University of California in San Diego presented a research which suggests that the activation of certain areas in the frontal lobes of the cerebral cortex correlates with mystical and religious perceptions. These data were confirmed by other researchers. The region detected in the brain is associated with both epilepsy and with intense religious perceptions. Activation of this area, named the "God module", is typical of people who suffer from the forms of epilepsy when they have visions of God and the sense of oneness with the Universe. This is the

[2] Crick F. The Astonishing Hypothesis. The Scientific Search for the Soul. A Touchstone Book. NY, 1995.
[2] Korotkov K., Williams B., Wisneski L. Biophysical Energy Transfer Mechanisms in Living Systems: The Basis of Life Processes. J of Alternative and Complementary Medicine, 2004, 10, 1, 49-57.

area of electrical activity in the brain, which occurs just before a person experiences an epileptic seizure, it also begins to activate when the person feels the presence of God. Dean Hamer, PhD, a behavioral geneticist who has worked at the National Cancer Institute (NCI) and the NIH, USA explains both seizures, and religious ecstasy, as a rapid transition of excitation between the two hemispheres of the brain with the resultant loss of sense of self-awareness and the sense of the presence of something much greater.

In order to investigate the "God module", Hamer had to identify and distinguish a particular group of those who could feel God's presence. He used the scale introduced by Robert Kieninger which measures the degree of transpersonal experience of the world. The scale of R. Kieninger has three levels:

1) a denial of self, a sense of belonging to something greater;

2) transpersonal identification (a sense of something that is associated with the world outside of oneself, love to the world, the desire to improve it, etc.);

3) a tendency to mysticism.

For people of these three types everything that is inexplicable and mysterious is exciting and attracts them more than the materialistic explanation of the world. Hamer noted that a high value on this scale is likely to be owned by people like Mahatma Gandhi, and the lowest values belong to the type of Genghis Khan.

Evaluating the data by this scale among the students of the United States and Australia, Hamer found that the feeling of the world's perception is substantially heritable, and the environment has very little effect on these estimates. Further, comparing the sense of perception and evaluation by this scale with an individual genotype, he identified the gene VMAT2, which is associated by this scale with self-negation stronger than with all the others, but still strong enough with all the three traits. A variant of this gene is the so-called spiritual alleles that control the monoamines chemically associated with the level of consciousness, and, interestingly, also with those substances that lead to mystical perception.

The most important of these chemicals is a neurotransmitter serotonin. Along with another neurotransmitter dopamine, it controls many psychological reactions of man, in particular, mood and the level of socialization. The level of neurotransmitters depends largely on genetics and consumed food. Therefore, some people have a positive attitude to life, while others are prone to complaints and depression. This led Hamer to the conclusion that a spiritual sense is rather an innate state of emotions than that of intellect. It may be inherent to some people, but is formed by others with great effort, and even then not in all cases.

Read biographies of the Fathers of Church. Many of them had mystical visions, talked with Jesus, Virgin Mary and angels. These visions arose spontaneously, without any effort and ceremonies of the believer and caused the strongest psycho-emotional reaction. Recall also the biography of Joan of Arc. The history also notes many cases of mass visions, especially in Catholic countries. At the same time, millions of believers with good intentions did not receive such grace. As noted by Hamer: "We do not know God, we feel Him".

Mystical sensations can be provoked or significantly enhanced with psychedelic drugs, both natural and synthetic. They are widely used by shamans and sorcerers. Studies have shown that these drugs cause a powerful eruption of neurotransmitters, particularly serotonin, which creates a feeling of euphoria, love for everybody. But, unlike the natural processes, artificial stimulation is inevitably accompanied by depletion of resources, which leads to breakdown and depression.

There was also found a correlation between the gene VMAT2, and a sense of belonging that relates to discipline, self-identity and ambitions. Hamer noted that people who have this gene active can be very high on R. Kleninger scale and can report about their out of body experience similar to feelings of those who took the drug Psilocybin. This is a very active element, called the "magician of fungi". Psilocybin activates the same receptors as serotonin and monoamine do. After further studies of the nature of this phenomenon, Dean Hamer wrote the book, where he relates certain genes with the perception of God.

Thus, it seems that some people get their mystical experience in a natural way, with a genetic pre-exposure from grandparents, while other must use pharmacology and fruits of plants. In this case, there may be the most unusual feelings. The neurologist Change Austin described the states of consciousness when time, fears and sensations of space were absolutely unfamiliar. It is attributed to the restructuring of the brain. In the normal state of man stable neural processes take place in the frontal lobes, which orientate him in space and determine the boundary between the body and the outside world, while the frontal and temporal lobes determine the proportion of time and support self-awareness.

Some people report transcendental perception of God's voice. In this case, Broca's area in the temporal lobe where the vocal sensations are located is activated when a person hears voices. During deep meditation, when the incoming sensory stimuli are suppressed, these inner voices can be easily faked and attributed to the source which is outside the body

Michael Persinger has demonstrated that mystical, psychic and paranormal perceptions are associated with a high mobility of nervous processes in the parietal regions. In fact, applying a weak magnetic field to the temples, he could induce a feeling of the out of body experience.

Finally, Hamer discusses relations between spiritual and religious perceptions. It is often expressed as: "I'm not a very religious person, but rather a spiritual one, and vice versa. Spirituality is based on consciousness, religiosity on perception. Spirituality is universal, it has its own culture; it has its forms and traditions. We can say that spirituality is genetically determined, whereas religiosity is based on culture, traditions, beliefs and ideas, i.e., in other words, one can learn to become religious. This is one of the reasons why spirituality and religiosity have a different impact on human lives and on society.

Examining the brain of monks during prayer and yogis during meditation neuroscientists have come to the conclusion that we can highlight certain areas of the cerebral cortex associated with transcendental sensations (feeling of flight, ecstasy, inner voices), but to explain the full range of emotional feelings and emotions, a sense of divine grace and joy by brainwork would be too strong a simplification.

Modern thinkers stand on the viewpoint of interaction. It describes a very subtle, sensitive way in which our consciousness, thoughts, emotions and our body, our brain and cells directly affect each other. As a simple example, we can say that when we experience joy this emotion involves our minds and our spirit, but at the expense of brain and nervous system activity there is a sharp release of certain neurotransmitters and their number grows in blood and the immune system, in the brain and body. And, accordingly, a decrease of the number of these cells can reduce our joyous state.

We also know that the use of our memory and capabilities of the brain leads us to keeping our nerve cells. It is possible to express this in the concept: use or lose. And, accordingly, the loss of the nerve cells over time affects memory and our ability. To say: Use your brain, but do not use your consciousness is the same thing to say as: Use your computer, but do not use the "Word" program. The capabilities of one system affect the capabilities of another one. Our mental software and our bodies is an indivisible unity when we talk about the union of structure and function. When the computer is turned off the program "Word" can not function, but when the computer is turned on it does not mean that it will use that program. We can say that consciousness is functioning and active only when the brain is alive and working. When the brain dies, consciousness can not function. But just because the brain is alive it does not mean that consciousness will be used to the maximum capacity.

Then what is Man, a complex biological machine, or a particle of God on Earth? Can we create a robot with consciousness, able to love, listen to music and enjoy the paintings made by Renoir?

Imagine that we have constructed a self-learning machine based on a super computer capable of performing certain actions to make improvements in its program depending on conditions and of transmitting the program to other machines. A community of such machines can build a factory for producing new, more sophisticated models and recycling of old ones, and in the course of their development it can form a quasi-stable structure. If only there is enough energy. We can see all the three signs of Darwinian triad. Can you recognize these machines alive? Is there a difference in their behavior from the colony of bees, ants or termites? It turns out there is.

Science has accumulated a huge number of observations indicating that within such concepts as "instinct", a "program of behavior" or "information at the genetic level" you can not explain the reality. In the beautiful book "From the Bee to the Gorilla" by Rémy Chauvin there is ample material leading to the statement: the behavior of animals indicates the presence of a phenomenon which biologists have identified by the concept of the "super-organism mind".

Now, here are more vivid examples.

Bees. *The dance language of bees.* It should be acknowledged that one of the most remarkable achievements of naturalists in recent decades is the discovery of the dance language of bees. Scout bees provide their countrymen with the detailed information about the holdings of nectar they have found, indicating the exact distance, direction, and the required number of gatherers.

Functional specialization. As long as there is the queen in a bee family, the ovaries of worker bees are not well developed; as soon as the queen disappears, the ovaries increase in size and develop so that they begin producing eggs.

The form of a honeycomb. The hexagon is a vessel with the highest capacity and the least expenditure of the material.

The art of building a honeycomb. Bees form a tight chain in which the temperature reaches 34 degrees. In this biological furnace the wax melts and turns into a regular geometric structure, with each worker bee knowing exactly where to put its piece of wax.

The memory phenomenon. It was found that bees of the two neighboring hives collect completely different pollen; and each hive keeps fidelity to the same species of plants for years. Thus, the hive that has collected pollen from the willow this year will stick to it in the next year, too. This is difficult to explain, because life of the worker bees is short, no more than one summer month, and those bees which have seen the blossoming limes this year will completely disappear by next summer. The only long-lived creature in the hive, the queen, does not leave the hive after her marriage flight and does not even feed on any pollen or nectar: the nurse bees feed her with jelly of their feeding glands.

Ants. *Unification of individual nests in the colony.* A colony is a stable union of several nests connected by roads and mastering the territory together. Ants, completely intolerant of outsiders, give a hearty welcome to any ant from their colony. It is like a Greek type of the state, a union of cities-policies.

The art of building the nest and keeping its dome clean and tidy. Ants grown in artificial conditions build a perfect ant-hill, although they have no one to learn from, and they have never seen what it is like.

Bringing up the new generation. The process of reproduction of ants is much more complicated than of insects-individualists. It includes breeding aphids, preservation of eggs in winter, feeding the youngsters, and then a rigid specialization of the rising generation. Some become soldiers and guard the ant-hill, some work inside the palace chambers, some run in the neighborhood.

Military actions, robbery, treachery and drunkenness in ant communities. (Well, just like people ...)

Little is known about the peculiarities of ant communities, such as growing mushrooms in underground greenhouses by the ant species Ana.

Termites. A nest of termites is a whole village. A nest found in Africa was larger than 100 m in diameter. A Belgian scientist **Dr. Denet** focused all his life on the study of the nests of African termites; looking at his pictures it is hard to believe that this is not the handiwork of a highly developed civilization. There are balls, basket-shaped and bell cupola, with walls consisting of rows of the ascending spiral columns, a complex system of galleries going into each other or intersecting. And everything is perfectly correct, as if carved. What is the significance of such a device, we still do not know, and it does not often happen that we can find the builders at their work. But this is not the point. We are interested in still the same old question, how can the tiny insects, without any plan, build their huge buildings, these pyramids and cathedrals of termites?

All the above and also numerous similar facts inexorably lead to the notion of the "superorganism mind", or the Collective Consciousness, guiding and managing the life of the population. Any individual member is like a cell of a single organism, an elementary source of the interference resonance structure of the common field of the population. Here we see a fundamental difference between bees and a plant of automatons.

The Collective Consciousness manifests itself most clearly by a example of ants, bees, termites or locusts, but it can also be seen in the behavior of more complex organized animals, especially social and gregarious.

Swallows and crows arrange their nests, guard their young, and defend their territory together warning the relatives with cries of the approach of enemies. In a poultry-yard, in a herd of monkeys, antelopes, or sea lions there is a strict social hierarchy and mutual help.

It would seem to be nice, but this strict system has its own pitfalls.

In the early XX century an American naturalist William Beebe came across a strange sight in the jungles of Guyana. A large group of ant-soldiers was walking around a huge circle. The circle was about 400 meters in circumference, and each ant took more than two hours to get around it. Thousands of ants kept going and going around the circle, it lasted more than two days, until most of them fell down dead. Biologists call this phenomenon the "circular mill". The mill occurs when the ant-soldiers designed to protect their colony from enemies find themselves away from home. When they get lost they follow the simple rule: follow the ant in front of you. Thus the mill comes into being interrupted only when some ant accidentally comes out of the circle and the others follow it.

There is another tragic example. Periodically, drawn by unknown signals, groups of whales or dolphins beach themselves, and all attempts to bring them back into the sea fail.

But doesn't it often happen with us humans, when detachments of soldiers go to meet their death on the orders of a tyrant? When the Individual Consciousness is completely suppressed in favor of the Collective, a society is formed, where all people vote by order and enthusiastically place in their offices the portraits of the leader. There are many examples in history; it would seem, people should learn from their mistakes, but no, it happens again and again. Periodically there are reports about religious sects whose members commit mass suicide at the command of their guru, or about the demonstrations of activists, nostalgically reminiscing about Stalin camps.

THE INDIVIDUAL AND COLLECTIVE CONSCIOUSNESS

We should strive to see in every thing what
nobody has seen and no one has yet thought over.

Georg Christoph Lichtenberg (1742-1799)

The notion of the "collective unconscious" was introduced into the science by Carl Gustav Jung (1875-1961), the prominent Swiss psychiatrist and founder of one of the areas of depth psychology, analytical psychology. Jung rejected the idea that personality is completely deterministic of its experience, training and environmental exposures. He believed that every individual is born with a "holistic personality sketch shown in potency since birth", and that "the environment does not give the individual an opportunity to become one, but only reveals what was already inherent in him".

Jung believed that there is some inherited mental structure having developed for hundreds of thousands of years, which makes us feel and realize our life experience in a well-defined way. And this certainty is expressed in what Jung called "archetypes" which influence our thoughts, feelings, actions

> *The Unconscious, as a set of archetypes, is sediment of all that has been experienced by mankind, up to its darkest origins. However it is not dead sediment, not an abandoned field of ruins, but a living system of reactions and dispositions, which in invisible, and therefore a more efficient manner, identifies an individual life.*
>
> *Jung K.G. The structure and dynamics of the Psyche.*
> *Problems of the Psyche of our time.*

"The collective unconscious is a reservoir where all the "archetypes" are concentrated. It involves implicit memory traces of the human past: the racial and ethnic history, as well as pre-human, animal existence. It is common human experience, characteristic of all races and nationalities. According to Jung, the theory of the collective unconscious explained both the appearance of ghosts in the mind of the medium, and disintegration of the schizophrenic's personality. Formerly people talked about the "demon possession" that came into the soul from the outside, but it now appears that their entire legion is already in the psyche. There is, according to Jung, a deep part of the psyche, which has a collective, universal and impersonal nature, the same for all members of this group. This layer of the psyche is directly connected with the instincts, i.e., heritable factors. They existed long before the appearance of consciousness and continue to pursue their "own" goal, despite the development of consciousness

Jung compared the collective unconscious with a matrix, a mushroom spawn (where a mushroom is an individual soul) with the underwater part of a mountain or iceberg: the deeper we go "under the water", the wider the base. From the common, family, tribe, nation, race, i.e., all humanity, we are going down to the heritage of pre-human ancestors. Like our body, the psyche is the result of evolution. Not only elementary behavioral acts, such as unconditioned reflexes, but also perception, thought, imagination are influenced by innate programs, universal examples. Archetypes are proto-forms of behavior and thinking. This is a system of aims and reactions, which imperceptibly determines a person's life.

The concept of the collective unconscious can be directly related to the notion of a collective or group consciousness. We have already discussed that the behavior of a group of people is fundamentally different from the behavior of each member of this group. The entire history of mankind is the history of large numbers of people. Civilization can be formed only when the number of people living together exceeds certain critical level. Civilization has always come into being in cities with a large number of farmers, ensuring that urban life. And as in all the processes the combination of the two elements is necessary: a tangible and an intangible:

•   The material side: there must be a developed agriculture for producing an excess product that can feed a crowd of rulers, warriors, servants, and citizens;

•   The spiritual side: there must be a developed religion for creation of a spiritual core of the society, enable to govern the people and direct their energy into big goals.

120

In the cities people closely communicate with each other, they are constantly exchanging information, and their whole life, their daily activity is synchronized, and is subordinate to a single rhythm. Is this a consequence of the information exchange in the form of conversations, newspapers, radio, television, or is there some other information medium of physical nature?

Can we talk about a Field of the Collective Consciousness as a physical category? What can we say about the fields?

MADNESS OF THE CROWD; WISDOM OF THE CROWD

> *How could it be that some sort of Hitler, some Dzhugashvili could govern eight million people? How did it become possible? Back in 1927 I brought this issue in the sociological background. I have long talked about this with Freud.*
>
> *Wilhelm Reich (1897-1957)*

In the mid 90-ies of the last century on the front pages of newspapers all around the world there appeared the reports on the atrocities of football fans. Crowds of fans crushed benches at the stadiums, like a live seething mass they poured onto the streets of towns and destroyed everything on their way. They were like a crowd of barbarians who seized a town. It did not depend either on the winning or losing of the favorite team, or country and nationality. The civilized-looking people turned into savages when they got into the Crowd. Special efforts required at the governmental level with the involvement of police units to place the process into some limits. For in every state it is understood that to raise the collective spirit, to build the sense of national identity, patriotism, the winning of the national team means much more than a hundred of newspaper articles.

However, football fanaticism is just one example of the madness of the crowd. If we look into the historical annals, it is easy to see that all the revolutions, rebellions, riots were manifestations of the spirit of madness that possesses people who gather in large groups. Each of them individually could be a normal rational person, but in the crowd wisdom disappeared, people forgot about their own interests, their own safety, and went together with the crowd to destroy, kill, rob, addressing their fury to their neighbor with whom they had lived side by side half their lifetime.

Tyrants and military leaders have always used this property of the crowd, and the ability to excite fury of the mob, and then send it in the right direction largely determines the success in battles. In a fit of a collective impulse people rushed at embrasures, spears and guns, not caring about their life, destroying the enemy; and the troops animated by the collective impulse defeated the enemy who was in many ways superior in his strength.

But woe is the commander if the crowd is in panic. As a single mass, it takes flight, often meeting its death. A regular army turns into a crazy crowd, and only some special situation, a powerful volitional impulse can stop this madness.

One of the first of who paid attention to these processes was the French psychologist Gustave Le Bon, who in 1895 published his book "The Crowd: A Study of the Popular Mind". Le Bon claims that the crowd is not just a sum of the constituent elements. It is somewhat an independent body. It has will and independence, and often does things that are not characteristic of each individual. Violence, aimlessness and lack of logic are the most typical properties of madness of the crowd.

As Henry David Thoreau put it, "The crowd never rises to the level of its best representatives, but on the contrary, degrades to the level of the worst".

Friedrich Nietzsche: "Madness is an exception for individuals, but the rule in groups".

A French psychologist Serge Moscovici in his book "The Age of Crowds" gave the following definition: "Crowds are gatherings of people who unite outside institutions and in spite of them on a provisional basis. In short, the crowd is anti-social and is formed in an anti-social manner. Crowds are mad. Madness is both in the indiscriminate movement of the masses who want to see a famous person, and in the crowd catching the man to be lynched, enduring his sentence, without being convinced of his guilt. These are massive invasions of the believers in the places where the miracle is to be seen.

The crowd, the mass is a social animal, torn off the chain. Moral prohibitions are swept off together with subordination to reason. The distinction between people blurs, and people splash out, often in violent acts, their passions and dreams: from low to heroic, from ecstasy to martyrdom".

Insane behavior is common both for human and animal crowds. A frightened herd of antelopes or bulls runs forward in a rush, hammering with their hooves those who have fallen, having no purpose and directed by no one. Madness captures the animals, the madness characteristic to a crowd of people, and this property comes from the ancient depths of the subconscious, the wild terror that lies in wait outside the walls of caves, in dark woods, from where one can escape only if getting lost in the crowd, and with the crowd attacking an unknown enemy, or those who represent it.

And in these subconscious fears one of the reasons of the crowd formation is the desire of people to be close to each other. As Baudelaire said in "Paris Spleen", "A lonely strolling and brooding man is attracted by an unusual delight of this universal uniting. Anyone who easily joins the crowd understands the feverish excitement which will never be accessible neither to a selfish man, locked like a trunk, nor to a lazy-bone, sitting in his shell like a shell-fish".

Most people reach out for a crowd, a group. It is especially pronounced in adolescence. Young people feel the need to belong to any group, to any team; it gives them the feeling of fullness of life, to be involved in something interesting and important. The values accepted in this group are much more important to them than what parents and teachers say. They tend to be not worse than others, and for this they are ready to make sacrifices and crimes, from tongue and cheek-piercing to aggression and robbery. Therefore it is so easy to organize communities of young people, carrying them away with some idea, be it political, religious or mystical. An experienced leader, generally, of older age, leads and directs the group, following his political, ambitious, or selfish interests. And this group, this crowd is becoming a powerful and dangerous force.

The MADNESS of the CROWD is one aspect of the collective consciousness. But there is still another one. It is the WISDOM of the CROWD. Psychologists have found that the average collective estimation and prediction of the collective in most cases works better than the judgments of experienced experts. In the book by James Surowiecki "The Wisdom of Crowds" there are numerous examples. Here is one of them.

On January 28, 1986 at 11.38 the Space Shuttle Challenger was launched from Cape Canaveral. After 74 seconds it reached an altitude of 15 km. The next moment it exploded. Reporting from Cape Canaveral went live, therefore the news of the disaster spread quickly. After 8 minutes the message was in the first few lines of the news of the New York financial exchange.

The market reacted immediately. In sight of everyone the stocks of the four main companies started falling; the companies that had provided the launch of "Challenger": "Rockwell International" who had built the ship itself and its main engines, "Lockheed", responsible for the terrestrial structures, "Martin Marietta", who produced the external fuel tanks; "Morton Thiokol" who had built the solid rocket booster. The fall of the shares was so rapid that the trades had to be interrupted for more than an hour. When trading resumed the shares of all four companies had fallen by 4-6%. "Morton Thiokol" suffered most of all, and by the end of the day its shares had fallen by 12%, while the remaining companies began a gradual increase, and by evening they had lost about 3%.

This means that the market almost immediately marked "Morton Thiokol" as the company responsible for the catastrophe. The value of shares of a company's stock is determined by how investors imagine the prospects of its future earnings. If such company suffers billions in losses due to disaster, if it loses its future orders, there will be no profit in the near future. A sharp fall in shares of "Morton Thiokol" compared with a slight drop in shares of other companies showed that investors intuitively laid the blame on it for the disaster.

It should be noted, however, that no official comment on the possible causes of the disaster was mentioned. This was not mentioned within six months during an official investigation. After lengthy investigations the Presidential Commission concluded that the cause of the accident had been the O-rings of the rocket booster. These rings should have prevented the side output of the hot fuel gases. Due to the frost the rings lost their properties, a leak was formed; the hot gases hit the main fuel tank, burned it and caused a huge explosion. The company "Morton Thiokol" was found guilty in the crash. The other three companies were fully justified.

In other words, half an hour after the explosion the exchange already KNEW who was responsible for the catastrophe, i.e., thousands of individual investors independently sensed what was happening, although there were no signs of it. Naturally, no one except a few specialists knew about the existence of the O-rings. Even the specialists of "Morton Thiokol" were not sure they were responsible for the catastrophe. This is evidenced by the fact that none of the staff of "Morton Thiokol" rushed to sell his shares. The exchange collectively came to the right decision, because this process complies with the basic rules of collective wisdom:

•   diversity of opinions (each person takes a decision based on his own idea about the company);

•   independence (decision of each does not depend on the opinions of others);

•   decentralization (people from different areas take part in the decision, each of them bases on his own   experience);

•   aggregation (there is a mechanism that generates the average estimate of the thousands of individual opinions).

Implementation of these rules is necessary for the team to take the right decision. In the case where there is an authoritarian leader or expert whose opinion prevails over all, the principle of collective wisdom is violated. The best group decisions are obtained when in the group there are disputes and disagreements, but not when there is general consensus and all people unanimously raise their hands not knowing really what it is all about. All attempts to create teams of experts or only top-level professionals prove ineffective, both in business and in sport. In particular, the presence of the "negligent pupil" in the group, who can hardly understand the essence of the discussion and asks "stupid" questions, dramatically increases the probability of obtaining the correct solution. Very often a new employee in a team trying to solve a challenging problem contributes to the achievement of success; and it is not because he or she is a super-expert, but because they can look at the problem at a different angle. In any large corporation there is its own Board of Directors, which invites people who do not belong to the corporation. Decisions of the Council determine the line of the company development.

Interestingly, the largest discrepancies between the opinions of individual experts and the opinion of the group appear in the predictions of the future. In the first part of the book we have already cited the examples of non-acceptance of new ideas and inventions. I would like to quote two other statements. Harry Warner, the Head and founder of the film company "Warner Brothers" in Hollywood have long resisted the introduction of the talking pictures. In 1927 he said in an interview, "Who the hell wants to listen to the chatter of actors?" President of the company «IBM» Thomas Watson said in 1943, "I think in the future there will hardly form a market for five computers". These words have laid the groundwork for the prosperity of Bill Gates, who believed in the future of computers and was able to conclude a very profitable deal for himself with IBM. He agreed that the company IBM will use only his software and he will receive interest from each computer sold. The contract was signed with ease, as nobody in IBM believed in the future of computing. When the sales exceeded over a million units a year, the company IBM tried to challenge the contract, but lawyers easily proved that it had been signed for all eternity.

However, as it turned out, group predictions are of much greater accuracy; however only if the group obeys the four mentioned above rules. The best examples are the so-called Electronic Opinion Markets. The idea was put forward by a group of scientists from the College of Business at the University of Iowa in the United States. In 1988 they organized an Internet site where anyone could participate in the prediction of presidential or gubernatorial elections in the U.S. On the basis of votes there was formed a score, which was constantly changing in real time. The idea was implemented as a stock exchange where participants could buy and sell "contracts" related to the chances of one candidate or another. This is the same principle as at an ordinary stock exchange where the shares of companies or contracts for the supply of raw materials are exposed.

For example, at the elections in California in 2003 a contract was offered, according to which a person could get $ 1 if Schwarzenegger won, and nothing in the event of loss. The contract value was constantly changing, reflecting the collective opinion of the likelihood of the candidate's winning. The cost of 50 cents meant that half of the participants did not believe in the victory of Schwarzenegger; 80 cents, meant that they estimated the chances of winning as 80%, etc. Thus, by buying 10,000 contracts at 80 cents a participant could win $ 2000. Naturally, people were attracted not so much by an opportunity to earn much but rather by an excitement of participation.

Analysis of the results of the predictions of the electronic stock exchange IEM showed that they were surprisingly accurate. For example, in recent years in 49 different elective activities, both American and foreign, the prediction accuracy ranged from 1.37% to 3.43%. 1.37% means that the market had predicted the candidate 48.63% of the vote, but he got 50%.The accuracy of these predictions has always exceeded the predictions of the most senior experts.

Following this example, other electronic stock exchanges were created where people can stake on sporting events, competitions and contests. In contrast to the bookmakers, where people stake only on the basis of their own predictions and these stakes are impossible to cancel, in the electronic exchange a participant monitors the result of the collective wisdom, and can instantly buy or sell the shares. The success of this idea is based on the four main principles:

- diversity of opinions;

- independence;

- decentralization;

- aggregation.

If at least one of these principles is forgotten, the collective wisdom turns into its opposite. And a striking example is the "pyramid schemes", so popular in our country, based on the principles of the "information cascade".

A classic example of such cascade is the construction of roads in the U.S. in the mid XIX century. The country rapidly developed, and it turned out that along with the railways there should be plenty of good roads linking small towns with the center. Asphalt at the time had not yet been invented, the construction of high-quality roads with sand and gravel was costly, and people moved along tracks that turned into mud flows after rain and were enveloped with clouds of dust in dry weather. Clearly such situation was not only in the U.S. but worldwide.

The engineer George Gedds proposed a solution of this problem. He proposed to build "wooden roads". Along the road down on the ground wooden beams were stacked and then lateral boards were nailed on them. It was quick and cheap. No preparation of ground was needed, no extra service. In the middle of XIX century when people went on foot or on horseback, such roads were greeted with enthusiasm. First, they were built around New York and after a short time they spread throughout the country. After 10 years more than 1000 companies in the U.S. were engaged in their construction.

However, the enthusiasm quickly ended. The predictions that the wooden roads would serve no less than 8 years did not materialize. 4 years later they came into complete disrepair, which made their construction unprofitable. Having rapidly spread throughout the country, they just as rapidly disappeared, together with the businessman who had created them.

The wooden roads are a classic example of an information cascade. The first roads were successful, as well as all the following ones constructed within a few years. This success inspired other people, they built their roads, and their neighbors, seeing the success of the venture, followed their example. Within a few years the wooden roads covered the entire country, and only after a long time the viciousness of the idea which was the basis of the entire project became clear; the wooden roads were very short-lived. (We do not mention even the fact that they would not suit the road transport: a horse can step over a broken board, but a motorist often will not notice it at all).

A cascade occurs when people send information to each other. Let's say, a group of tourists in an unfamiliar city has decided to go to a restaurant. They ask for advice from a clerk. He encourages them to his uncle's restaurant, although in reality it is not the best place in town. Other tourists passing them by on the street and comparing the crowded hall of the restaurant with half-empty halls of the neighboring restaurants make the same choice. Then both groups recommend the restaurant to their uncle's neighbors in the hotel, and the latter do the same sending the message to other people. Thus, the information cascade forms, and the owner of the restaurant gets his profit.

A sadder example is financial pyramids. The first investors get good interest rates, they spread the news about an easy income to their friends, the number of contributors is growing exponentially, the circulating money supply increases, the organizers may pay more interest, it attracts new investors, and the process is growing, until thee moment when the whole pyramid collapses. It is inevitable, because otherwise at a certain moment the volume of payments should exceed the revenue, and no business can provide the claimed high interest rates.

It is surprising that after the collapse of the first gigantic pyramid schemes people continue to believe in this idea and bring their money to the Field of Boobies. And they do it quite willingly. In recent years, the organizers of pyramid schemes increasingly often do it under the camouflage of religious, psychological or business groups, using NLP techniques to recruit new members, but their essence remains the same: taking money from dupes, using the laws of the psychology of crowds.

As we see, even from several presented cases, the knowledge of these laws is becoming more necessary for leaders of all levels: from managers of large enterprises to presidents. Major political leaders have always understood the importance of operating with the crowd and enjoyed it in their work. Lenin's popularity was largely based on his public speeches; Stalin created a special system where participation in public events, such as meetings and demonstrations was mandatory for all citizens. Hitler could speak for hours in front of the crowds of his followers; the same explains the popularity of Fidel Castro and his modern follower Hugo Chavez. Social psychology deals with this issue, however, recently we observe the growing recognition of the fact that along with verbal and visual communication the field component is of great importance in shaping the mood of the crowd. We can talk about the Group Field, the Morphogenetic Field, the Biological field, this concept is not uniquely identified, but the field is the basis of the crowd's behavior as a whole, as an organism, whose behavior is not confined to the behavior of its individual cells. Consequently, we can speak about individual and collective consciousness.

WHAT IS CONSCIOUSNESS?

"I sent my Soul through the Invisible,
Some letter of that After-life to spell:
And by and by my Soul return'd to me,
And answer'd "I Myself am Heav'n and Hel"

Omar Khayyam (1048-1131)

A worker on an assembly line, at first glance, behaves in the same way as an ant. However, this is only a superficial similarity. The assembly line for a worker is only one of his numerous functions: he can also be the caring father of a family, a fisherman, a collector, a reader of novels, a spectator, or a member of a political party. When conditions change, the worker can respond irrespective to his work program, and even in spite of it. The worker can go on strike and demand changing his conditions. We know nothing about the strikes of ants. Therefore, it is beneficial to replace the worker with a robot, whose behavior is fully consistent with the ant psychology.

It is noteworthy that the rigid structure of a collective, being surprisingly stable for ants and having ensured their survival for hundreds of millions of years with all the changes of the environment, turned to be totally unsustainable for the human society; even being forcibly established and guarded, it spontaneously disintegrates in a historically short term. The socialist system existed for 70 years, and quietly broke up without any pressure from outside. It is obvious that with the suppression of the Individual Conscience in the name of the Collective in the human society the fundamental laws of life of the noosphere, the laws of the stability of a complexly organized system are violated. The Communist model of the structure of a society is perfect for protozoa and insects; however, all attempts of introducing it for people, the beings with a more complex organization, are not viable.

All the above makes us change our views on the structure of the human mind: much of what we refer to the unconscious is associated with super-Consciousness.

In addition, it makes us look differently at the definition of the concept of "consciousness". This notion is one of the main areas of

THE ENERGY OF CONSCIOUSNESS

sciences related to man. The basic concepts of any scientific theory are primary, i.e., are not defined in terms of other previously introduced concepts, but are introduced intuitively. They define the whole future course of the possible arguments, remember how different are the geometry of Euclid and Lobachevsky- Riemann, with different primary definitions.

The history of the attempts to build a rigorous, not intuitive definition of consciousness is rooted in the distant past. Moreover, all these attempts are inevitably based on an a priori division of the whole nature into the conscious and the unconscious: the definition should only formally draw this border exactly where expected. Depending on this, the authors of the concept make statements about the adequacy of the specific wording. Definitions based on this division, are subjective and, moreover, biased, most often in favor of Homo sapiens. With this approach to avoid the logical tautology is not possible in principle.

Furthermore: being the foundation for experiments, such approach to the definition of consciousness methodically leads to incorrect results. Thus, in the well-known experiment the experimenter removes the bell from the entrance to the wasp nest, and the wasp completes a new one. Further, he makes a hole in the tube bend before the bell, and the wasp builds both the tube, and the bell. "Aha!" says the experimenter, "Now you see, the wasp has no reason!" But if aliens, as an experiment, make a hole in somebody's trousers over and over again, the person will first try to patch them, then he will buy new pants, but eventually he will kick them out of the window, swearing and pounding his feet. "Aha!" the alien will say, "Now you see, Man has no reason!"

The reason here is that we assume a priori which behavior is reasonable and which is not. Making experiments not on ants and wasps, but on a man working on an assembly line you can get no less strong evidence that he is no more than a biorobot. The entertainment industry and a TV program guide can provide us with even more impressive indication of the total lack of human reason.

But if we can easily agree that it is impossible to study the mind and emotional world of a man examining his behavior through the reaction to a failure of the assembly line, why do we deny the same for ants, bees, termites, etc.?

131

Obviously, even just a transition to micro-or macro-world is accompanied by changes in ideas about what consciousness is, as it is difficult to talk about any expected behavior. People's behavior on the streets of the city observed from a bird's-eye in an expedited fashion is strangely reminiscent of an anthill or a beehive.

These arguments inevitably lead us to a contradiction: an intuitive introduction of a term suggests that its meaning is equally understood by all who use the relevant theory. The concept of consciousness is complex enough already to demand to express itself (I can not but recall the famous theorem of Gödel's Incompleteness of formal systems, which establishes the impossibility of judging the properties of a system by means of the system).

At the same time in everyday life, we define the concept clearly enough. We say:

• "a conscious man" about the individual who understands the nature of his actions and their possible consequences. From this perspective, neither a drunkard, nor a criminal can be attributed to conscious people. Their behavior is contrary to the moral standards of society. Thus, we see that the term "conscious" has a moral and ethical connotation and refers to people who understand and control their behavior in society. At the same time:

• an "unconscious behavior" is the state when a person acts without controlling his actions and does not understand their consequences.

A whole range of states can be between these two extreme situations. One popular option is when a person is aware of all that happened, but acts in a completely unexpected way, both to him and to others. For example, spouses during a family quarrel can tell each other such things, for which they will be very embarrassed. In a crowd of fans a man can cry, fight and smash benches, although in real life he is quite a peaceful citizen. Another extreme is the phenomenon of "out of body experience" when a patient being on the operating table under general anesthesia, watches everything that is going on as if taking a detached view.

Thus, to avoid all these difficulties, in modern science it is customary to speak of a "normal" awaken consciousness and various deviations from this state. In psychology it is customary to operate the concepts of "subconscious" and "superconscious", but we will put aside the discussion of these definitions. Thus, the "normal" consciousness is the individual's ability to perceive events and respond in accordance with the level of socio-cultural environment.

Hence, is consciousness associated with the level of social development? Yes, of course. For the man of XIII the appearance of a living dragon would be perceived as something natural, though with fear. We can assume that in those times dragons were common wild animals, like wolves or bears. These dragons crawled in those times, and now they preserved only on the island of Komodo. For a modern man the appearance of a dragon will be perceived as a hallucination, or as part of Disneyland.

In this context, the definition of "consciousness" should not be viewed as an attempt to constructively identify this philosophical category, but as a way to agree on the meaning embedded in the concept. It can be understood as the coordination of intuitive ideas, a sort of "check of the clocks".

In our studies we use the following definition:

Consciousness is a property (ability) of the objects of nature to form abstract representations of the outside material world, suitable for use in purposeful activity through sensory perception.

The more we perceive the world around us, the more it startles us by its complexity. The boundaries of our knowledge are continuously moving aside, making the process of cognition in the ongoing race beyond the horizon. On this way, many obvious and universally accepted theses periodically become paradoxical and ambiguous; many representations die or radically change. The true way of all science goes through crises and paradigm shifts to new crises. This path is endless, convoluted and tortuous, but there is no other way.

A direct mechanical transfer of representations from the ant-hill to human society is impossible; however, the study of these "parallel worlds" can give the same long-anticipated push for a new round of the development of science predicted by many scientists of the planet.

Consciousness is the ideal category, the basic imperative along with Matter and Information. We can on the basis of this definition only detect signs of its presence.

It is possible to introduce the definition of "Consciousness" from other considerations, based on the principles of **synergetics.**

Consciousness is an ability of a system to make a deliberate choice at the point of bifurcation of one of the possible ways of development, according to the criterion of optimality in terms of achieving the global attractor through a chain of local ones.

"That's too technical and confusing and unclear!" the dear reader will exclaim. And he will be right. We will not even discuss this definition not to delve into the scientific wilderness. Let's talk about one important concept, the Altered State of Consciousness.

WHAT IS ALTERED STATE OF CONSCIOUSNESS ?

With the thoughts I'd be thinkin'
I could be another Lincoln,
If I only had a brian.

E.Y. Harburg (1898-1981)

Imagine a student busy preparing for a serious test; a scientist solving an important scientific problem; a composer or artist, working over another masterpiece. Such person does not notice anything around him, he is completely immersed in his process, and at some point a period of enlightenment comes, and the whole pages of a complex text remain in memory, words, music and images are born as if by themselves, and he only need time to transfer them onto paper or canvas. Moreover, often to achieve the optimal creative state certain specific conditions are required: for somebody it is solitude in the quiet of his apartment or a forest hut, for another person it is music, for the third one a glass of brandy. And an absolutely necessary condition is full immersion in the subject of his activities. If you constantly respond to telephone calls and count the flies on the ceiling nothing will happen.

All the above examples are characterized by man's coming into the ASC.

To the Altered States of Consciousness (ASC) we relate various states of man when his perception of the reality is not adequate to the social norms. Say, a loving couple is walking hand in hand and does not notice nothing and nobody around. It is a typical Altered State of Consciousness, available, however to few. Or, an opera soloist enters the stages, begins singing, and the audience forget about time and space, they are fully charmed by the music. It is the Altered State of Consciousness. An artist paints a picture and can stay for many hours without food and water. It is the Altered State of Consciousness. A mountaineer during the ascent endures cold and loadings due to which all his physiological functions should terminate. All these are examples of the Altered State of Consciousness. We say "altered" because such state of consciousness is not characteristic of everyday life and most people never experience it. However, as we will show in this chapter, the Altered State of Consciousness is accessible practically to anyone. All you need is to want it so much and to try hard. Nowadays there are special methods teaching to come into such states, they have a common name "mental training".

Another example: a shaman goes into a trance and, spinning and rocking in the smoke of burning herbs, foresees the future or exorcises.

There is another important and interesting area of the Altered Consciousness, the sport of the highest achievements.

It is proved that the outstanding athletes during a competition go into the Altered State of Consciousness. Often you can hear from sports reports: "The excitement did not allow the athlete to perform in full force". Alas, this is the evidence of incompetence, poor psychological preparation. What's the use of wasting time and efforts in training if you can not show your potential during the competition? A good coach, in addition to physical strength and skill, will work on sporting spirit of his wards. In martial arts this factor is one of the highlights of training. Using various techniques, the Master teaches the Disciple the transition into the Altered State of Consciousness. It is in this state that you can break bricks with your hand and feel the enemy with your back.

Studies have shown that ASC is characterized by a special state of brain, body and energy activity. The figure (Fig. 28) shows a schematic diagram of Altered States of Consciousness. It shows that the body should be relaxed, but ready to act as a cocked trigger. As fencers say, you must hold the sword in your hand as a small bird, if you loosen the grip it will fly away, if you grip it stronger it will suffocate. Tension, stiffness, fear do not allow us to go into the Altered State of Consciousness. The body must be calm, but with a high level of internal energy, ready for implementation. The brain must be active, but without anxiety or tension. Transition into to the Altered State of Consciousness is abrupt, just in a single elusive moment.

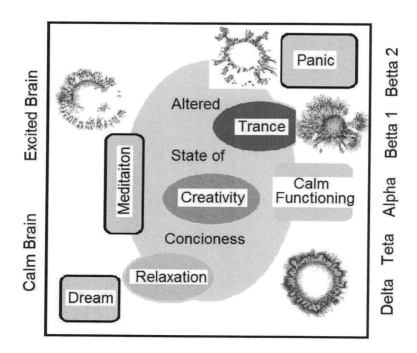

Fig.28. Schematic diagram of Altered States of Consciousness

The nature of the brain electrical activity in the Altered State of Consciousness changes compared with the usual condition or sleep. The low-frequency b-activity is suppressed; the brain begins to generate higher frequencies. Interestingly, the dependence of the amplitude of brain waves on the frequency decreases, which in the Altered State of Consciousness, with certain accuracy, can be approximated by the "golden section". This relationship discovered by the ancient Greeks is the basis of harmony between nature and classical architecture. We can say that in the Altered State of Consciousness the brain reaches a more harmonious state.

This is manifested in the distribution of neural activity over the surface of the brain, studied with the help of modern programs of mapping the brain activity. If in the normal waking state we observe the activity in only some areas of the brain, predominantly frontal, then as a person goes into the Altered State of Consciousness the activity is distributed throughout the cerebral cortex, covering the two hemispheres. The brain starts to work harmoniously as a whole, including all of its structures into a single wave symphony, washing the surface of the brain, such as the surf washes the coastal rocks.

Now, this special state of activity does create visions, unusual sensations and feelings. The question arises: the feeling of exaltation, Divine communion, prayer ecstasy, what is it, a byproduct of the special status of the cerebral cortex, stimulation of certain cortical areas that are not involved in ordinary life activity, or is it connection to data fields, adjustment of the systems to the "music of the spheres"? Currently, these questions have no answer. Experimental data are still very few, and they can be interpreted differently, depending on the predilections of the interpreter. The physiological point of view is that human behavior is determined by the nature of the activity of certain parts of the nervous system, and all our emotions are nothing more than a reaction to external and internal stimuli, taking into account the innate biological needs. Love is a modified sexual desire, the instinct of procreation; aesthetic pleasure from art, music, theater is a consequence of stimulation of certain brain regions, developed in the course of training and learning, prayer and meditation are the specific relaxation exercises.

It is currently difficult to oppose something serious to these theses. Experimental data, including the discussion in this book can be interpreted in different ways. But somehow we do not want to believe that all our spiritual aspirations and values, all the cultural achievements of mankind is nothing more than a product of physiological acts. Can it be that the music of Mozart, Shostakovich, or The Beatles is just a byproduct of abnormal brain activity of genius, similar to abundant salivation of a hungry dog? Can it be that the great temples and mosques were built for the convenience of collecting money from the working people doped by "the opium of religion"?

Then why do millions of people still come to the concert halls and churches in search of peace and spiritual harmony?

I believe that a person has special qualities in comparison with the rest of the animal world, and the centrifugal development of our civilization is a manifestation of the global process of the growing Collective Consciousness of Humanity, unfolding in its potential power in space and time of our Universe. For thousands of years fighting and suffering, building and destroying, we are going through the stages of historical development, gradually maturing, realizing the depth of our spiritual essence, and just wondering about our global mission.

At the same time, the Altered State of Consciousness is not only ecstasy and a sense of harmony, in some cases, this state can be dangerous. Often the nature of brain activity in the Altered State of Consciousness is similar to its activity during epileptic seizures. The difference is that a person goes into the Altered State of Consciousness by his will and, in principle, is able to quit it (though not always quickly and easily), while the epileptic activity arises spontaneously and often ends with a seizure. As the great Salvador Dali said, "My only difference from a madman is that I'm not crazy".

But if one can not quit it, what then? Then the man is doomed to the existence of a deranged, he begins to live in a world of dreams and sensations, not having contact with the outside world. Thus, mental training, astral travel outside the body, the transition to the Altered State of Consciousness should be treated cautiously. There is a chance that once there will be no return.

What does it depend on? Why can one deeply immerse into transpersonal depths and another will lose his mind and never recover? It depends on the individual characteristics of the structure of the neural network of the cerebral cortex, which is determined by the genetics and the first years after birth. This is physiology. We are different in digesting food, processing alcohol, and generating emotions. At the present time it is impossible to predict the features of these processes. We can only observe and draw conclusions.

In addition to the brain's electrical activity in the Altered State of Consciousness, the nature of induced emission processes, the parameters of GDV-activity also changes. On the very first stages of research it was found that the patterns (images) of fingers glow change. The images on Fig. 29 show the nature of these changes, they become more broken, lose shape and power. It was later discovered that this is due to a glow decrease in the visible region and an increase of the ultraviolet (UV) component. But the ultraviolet light means higher frequencies! Consequently, we can say that in the Altered State of Consciousness the frequency of the emitted light increases! During meditation, prayer man' glow emits at higher frequencies! Isn't it a nice life-affirming conclusion!

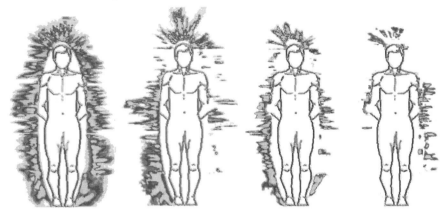

Fig.29. Transformation of the Energy Field in the transition to Altered States of Consciousness

At the same time, many people in the Altered State feature peculiar glow in the form of double rings or spaced spots, around the fingers. (Fig. 30) Moreover, these typical images can remain for a long time, as long as the person remains in the Altered State of Consciousness. We will not go into technical details, but a plausible explanation can be that this is a transition of the organism into a coherent state, where the systems and organs begin to work in a consistent mode in resonance with each other, and the emission acquires coherent properties, like a laser beam. That is, we do not just glow, but we send laser pulses into space!

Another feature of the Altered State of Consciousness is an increase in the GDV glow over time. In the normal state the signal of GDV glow subsides a bit in the beginning, and then remains almost constant, more or less strongly fluctuating around a constant level. By the way, the nature of these fluctuations depends on the level of stress, which enables us to evaluate the stress by the dynamics of the GDV signal.

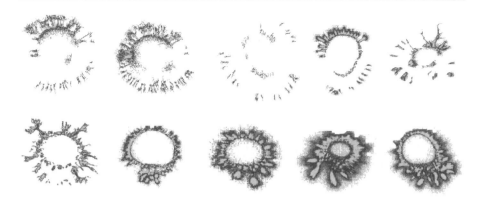

Fig.30. EPI images of fingers in the state of Altered States of Consciousness

Studying the Altered State of Consciousness we were surprised to see that the GDV signal grows in time! (Fig. 31)

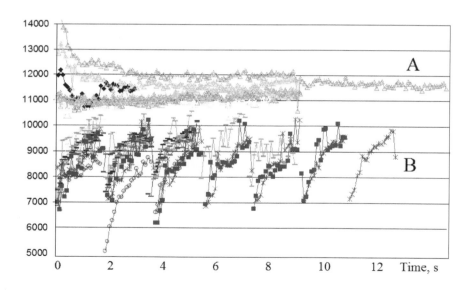

Fig.31. Time dynamics of a person's Energy:
A – in normal state; B – in Altered States of Consciousness

When similar measurements were repeated for dozens of people, it became clear that this is not an accident. Indeed, in the Altered State the energy increased sharply in time! How can this be explained? What are the mechanisms to associate it with?

The first analogy came from Chinese traditional medicine. One of its foundations is the notion of the energy channels, meridians, penetrating all the organs and systems and implementing energy circulation throughout the body. The endpoints of the meridians are located on fingers, therefore, when we measure the finger glow, we "connect" to the energy channels. Now imagine that we "pump the energy" from a channel with a certain diameter. Clearly, we obtain a constant flow in time, or a continuous signal. If the channel has no energy, the signal decreases, which is observed in the case of various diseases. Now imagine that in the process of the Altered State of Consciousness more and more channels open in this channel, like rivulets from the earlier closed sources start to flow into it. The energy flow increases, and we observe a sharp increase of the signal in time.

Later a biophysical concept was also developed: the energy transfer is associated with the transport of electronically excited states in the chains of protein molecules. This idea is based on the latest ideas in quantum biophysics, mainly of Russian scientists. The electron transfer does not require any special individual channels or conductors; electrons form temporary "paths", like ants' paths in the forest. That's why no one could detect specific structures corresponding to the meridians and acupuncture points. These are virtual paths, emerging and disappearing as needed. Their main carrier is, apparently, the connective tissue and the bone structures. The flows of the transported electrons are determined by distribution of potential fields in the body depending both on physiological and mental activity.

THE FIELD APPROACH

> *Now, my own suspicion is that the universe is not only queerer than we supposed, but queerer than we can suppose.*
>
> *J.B.S. Haldane (1892-1964)*

The physical fields, in the modern view, are a special form of matter, a physical system possessing an infinite number of degrees of freedom. The examples of physical fields can be electromagnetic and gravitational fields, the field of nuclear forces, as well as wave (quantized) fields corresponding to different particles.

The concept of a field (electric and magnetic fields) was first introduced by a brilliant physicist Michael Faraday in the 30-ies of XIX century. He regarded the concept of a field as an alternative to the theory of a long-range action, i.e., interaction of particles at a distance without any intermediate agent (thus was interpreted, for example, the electrostatic interaction of charged particles according to Coulomb, or the gravitational interaction of bodies under the law of universal gravitation by Newton). In the 60-ies of XIX century *J. K. Maxwell* developed the idea of Faraday's *electromagnetic field*, and formulated his laws in the form of Mathematical Equations. Since then, the field concept has become a basis of modern science.

According to the field concept, the particles involved in any interaction (e.g., electromagnetic or gravitational), create at each point of the space around them a special state, a force field, which manifests itself in a force effect on other particles that are placed in some point of this space. Originally, a mechanistic interpretation of the field as elastic stresses of the hypothetical medium, the "ether" was set forward. However, giving the "ether" the properties of an elastic medium was in sharp contrast with the results of later experiments. From modern viewpoint, such mechanistic interpretation is senseless, since the elastic properties of macroscopic bodies are completely explained by electromagnetic interaction of particles from which they consist. The relativity, having rejected the concept of the "ether" as a special elastic medium, gave a fundamental meaning to the notion of

Field as a primary physical reality. Indeed, according to the relativity, the propagation velocity of any interaction can not exceed the velocity of light in vacuum. Therefore, in the system of interacting particles the force acting at this moment of time on a particle of the system is not determined by the arrangement of other particles at the same moment, i.e., the change of the position of one particle has an effect on another particle not at once but after a certain period of time. Thus interaction of particles whose relative velocity is comparable with the velocity of light can be described only through the fields created by them.

Physical fields not only implement interactions between particles; there can exist and manifest free **physical fields** independent from the particles that created them (for instance, electromagnetic waves). Therefore, it is clear that **Physical fields** should be regarded as a special form of matter. Experience showed that (first for electromagnetic field) energy and impulse of the field vary in a discrete way, i.e., a **physical field** can correspond to certain particles (e.g., photons to electromagnetic field, gravitons to gravitational field). This means that description of a **field** with the use of field functions is just an approximation with a certain area of application. Quantum mechanics proves that a system of interacting particles can be described by a quantum field. Thus, not only certain particles correspond to each field, but vice versa, quantized fields correspond to all known particles. This fact is one of the manifestations of wave-particle duality of matter. Quantized fields describe the destruction (or creation) of particles, and at the same time the emergence (annihilation) of antiparticles. Such field is, for example, the electron-positron field in quantum electrodynamics.

In the recent several decades physicists have not stopped trying to create a general, unified field theory. It is expected to describe all these fields as different manifestations of the one, the "common physical field".

The field concept turned to be so important to describe the interactions in physics that, by analogy with it, the concepts of information, semantic fields were introduced. You should not confuse them with physical fields. They have no clear physical media. It is a convenient way to describe various interactions.

It should be remembered, that a physical field is not available to direct perception, and is detected only through its effects on other physical objects. It is impossible to directly measure electric or magnetic field. You can only observe its influence on some physical processes: for example, rotation of the magnetic needle, or the strength of the current in the sensor. Let us recall the school experiment with iron filings, manifesting magnetic field, or heaviness in the arm from the weight, which manifests gravitational field.

The concept of biological fields was launched in the mid 30-ies by an outstanding Russian scientist Alexander Gurvich. The idea is that in addition to the physical-chemical level, a system of fields distributed in space is bound with every biological object. Gurvich wrote,

"The concept of cells interaction is confined to the creation of a synthesized field, whose properties essentially match the cellular margins, and which has always belonged to the whole and was characterized by geometrical parameters. If a healthy cell becomes sick, then at a certain stage of pathogenesis it may change the type of its biofield to the opposite. With a proper therapeutic effect on the organism and, in particular, on the biofield of a sick man, cells again go into their original (basic) vector orientation.

Thus, Gurvich showed that biological field is the basis for maintaining life of the organism as a whole. The daughter of Alexander G. Gurvich Anna, analyzing her father's works noted,

"In living systems there is a continuous conjugate dependence between different levels. The whole (actual field) normalizes the spatial parameters of the processes at the cellular and molecular levels and, in its turn, depends on the frequency of occurrence and distribution of the elementary fields (molecular acts) and cell fields, representing their geometrical synthesis".

By the end of the twentieth century biological field has been strongly associated with electromagnetic field, although for decades there were active discussions about the possible existence of some other fields. The most advanced was the notion of **torsion fields**, developed by a team led by Anatoly Akimov, but they were not able to convince the scientific community of the importance of their ideas. Electromagnetic field is generated by the motion of electric charges. In the body a variety of electrical processes is continuously proceeding, ranging from

144

the level of cells to the level of individual systems and organs. Electromagnetic field is associated with each of these processes. As academician Yu. Gulaev noted,

"Around any biological object during its life a complicated picture of physical fields emerges. Their distribution in space and change in time provide the important biological information that can be used, in particular, in medical diagnosis".

Fields of different systems and organs in the body are coherent, i.e., synchronized in their activity. This leads to their forming a total field with interference or, in other words, holographic properties. The idea of the coherence of electromagnetic field of the body is actively developing in modern biophysics, for example, in Germany by F. Popa's team, in Italy by Del Guidicci's and in many other universities and research centers. The interference or holographic field has very interesting properties; it carries information about the object that created it in each of its particles. This means that if such field is recorded on a hologram, and then when the holographic plate breaks, each fragment will carry information about the whole object. Isn't it just like the magic mirror from Andersen's fairy tales?!!

Holographic principles were laid in 40-ies of the late century by Dennis Gabor and subsequently led to the development of lasers and holographic technology. At the same time, these ideas can be fully applied to a biological organism. We can say that the field level is the base level of the control of biological systems. This level was implemented in the most primitive biological objects long before the formation of vegetative and central nervous system. This level determines the functioning of the system as a whole; it is the level of the coherent interaction of different parts.

We have put forward the concept that the acupuncture points are a projection of the wave quantum fields on the skin surface. At the same time, from the principle of field structures, it is obvious that the field extends outside the body, theoretically, to an infinite distance. Thus, information about the state of the organism can theoretically be obtained at very large distances from it. The field structure of the body determines the processes of morphogenesis, i.e., the development process of the organism; it also determines the existence of the organism as a single system. Disorders at any level will show, primarily the loss of control of the body over its individual parts, which leads to systemic diseases. Gurvich's ideas were later developed into the concept of morphogenetic fields of Sheldrake and subsequently led to the concept of the holographic structure of brain and body.

If we accept the idea of the field of an individual organism, individual person, then we can talk about the collective field; beginning from the level of the family, workplace, nation, religious denomination, to the level of humanity. With each of these levels different spatial field structures are associated. Thus, the exchange of information and influence of one person on another is, among other things, at the field level.

As we have already noted, in medicine it has only recently been recognized that our feelings, emotions and spiritual experiences are not only important, but also a decisive moment in our lives and health. The acceptance of these ideas requires taking the next step: to return to the holistic conception of the essence of human nature. Man is not only a physical body capable of producing ideas, just as the liver produces bile, but he is a triple, single entity: the physical body + consciousness, thought, emotions, information structure, + the supreme being. In other words: body, soul and spirit.

The physical body belongs to the material world and obeys its laws. The information structure that can be associated with the soul is a field structure, and we apply to it the laws that we use to describe the fields. We can say that the information field is a vector, i.e., has a certain direction in space. It has the source, it is man himself, and it is spread from this source in all directions. This field can be directed in a certain way, i.e., focused in one direction or another, it can be scattered in space and, being coherent to the fields of other people, can interact with them.

At the same time it must be borne in mind that it is not a physical field, it is a description of the interaction process.

We can say that the information field is a continuously changing shell that exists around a man, but, unlike radio, this field depends not only on the person, but on everything around him. The information field is very sensitive to any changes in the environment and to a large extent depends on the interaction with fields of other people. Thus, it is our delicate shell that carries information about the person and tunes to the world around us depending on all its changes.

Information fields of individuals and groups of people add up to and create the collective information field, which exists as an independent structure, evolving, becoming more complicated and imprinting all the events in this collective information field. Anybody can have access to this information field, receiving information from it. All new ideas mature, crystallize in this field and incarnate (verbalize) in the minds of individuals. Not without reason new discoveries, inventions, whose time has come, which the humanity is ready for, often simultaneously occur to people in different countries, in different parts of the earth. Thus, interaction of the individual with the information field takes place, and every person is a generator of information coming into this field, and everyone at the same time takes information from this field. This field is a link of the individual and the universal spirit. Therefore, an individual can reach his highest achievement being a part of the world spirit and, having verbalized some idea and made it available to others, to embody it in his information field. The concept of the threefold manifestation of human nature makes it possible to move from a primitive model of man as a biological machine, to the notion of man as the quintessence of the Divine Spirit. Characteristically, these ideas have direct parallels in the modern scientific concepts, in particular, the quantum field theory.

In the same hierarchy we see the transition from the material forms of life to the field, information ones. Therefore, when we talk about metaphysical levels we introduce into consideration the next layer of reality which is not material, but based on different forms of the existence of matter. This is the level of super-physical, the level of the ideal, the level of Soul and Spirit. It is the highest level in our hierarchy, and at the same time it is the foundation of everything. Thus, it appears that this level is based on all the previous ones, and at the same time it is their foundation. During the deployment of the Spirit He came to a certain stage of self-expression, and presented one of his infinite entities in the form of matter. Matter in the process of self-development came to the creation of the mind and to the moment of awareness of the Spirit. The Spiral closed. Therefore, we can talk about the closure of the levels of their folding into a spiral, having neither end nor beginning, like the Moebius ring. In whatever point of this ring we step, we can obtain information on all the underlying levels. In principle, on the overlying, as well. We should only be able to ask a question, to find a method of an integrated approach.

Of great interest is to investigate not only an individual field, but its connection with the collective fields. The figure shows the scheme of the Individual and Collective lines of development in Space and Time. As seen from this scheme, the main development of Man is on the path of collective processes: for millions of years the physical appearance of Homo Sapiens has hardly changed, we look the same and have the same personal striving as an inhabitant of Ancient Egypt and Mesopotamia, but how much the status of the collective has changed! During an insignificant historical period this status has undergone great changes, from group cannibalism to modern humanistic society. That is why we so often see the echoes of this ancient cannibalism in our life. But the collective development can be clearly seen in the historical perspective, and it continually goes on: up to a planetary status, accessing the Universal Information Field of the Collective Intelligence, provided by the regulated Altered States of Consciousness. Not the space flights of frozen astronauts of hundreds years of duration, but the information inter-cosmos and inter-galaxy contacts outside time and distance, this is the future of mankind! We will be members of the galactic union, but it will happen not on a physical but on the information level!

A new element that emerged in the course of life on Earth was the appearance of the elements of the Individual Consciousness in animals. In the evolutionary process it emerged much later than the Collective Consciousness. It looks as if nature had achieved perfection in the development of collective organisms, and they took their stable niche in the biological life, and after that the Individual Consciousness began to develop. The highest stage of this process is Homo Sapiens whose distinctive features are both the developed Individual Consciousness and the highly organized Collective Consciousness.

In modern science there is a concept of the **BIFURCATION POINT**. This is the moment in development when there is a choice of one of several ways.

If you go to the right, you will lose the horse,

If you turn to the left, you'll lose your sword,

If you go straight, you'll lose your life.

It is a typical example of a bifurcation point (although very sinister). In our life we have repeatedly faced with a choice:

Should I go after school to college or work?

Should I marry Kolya or Sasha?

Should I stay at this work or look for a new one?

Each moment of decision is the point of bifurcation. We define our lives for the next period, and it is difficult to know in advance how well the choice was made.

The concept of bifurcations is applicable to any processes in the Universe. For example, we can speak about bifurcation stages of the evolution of the Noosphere:

• the stage of division of biological life from the inert nature and evolutional complication of the forms of this life;

• the stage of formation of biological structures characterized by the Collective Consciousness in the absence of the Individual Consciousness;

• the stage of evolutionary complications of biological structures without the Collective Consciousness and the emergence of the elements of the Individual Consciousness in them;

• the emergence of the biological species with both well-developed Individual Consciousness and the Collective Consciousness.

It is obvious that at any evolutionary stage the species emerged, being in equilibrium with the environment and more or less flexibly reacting to its changes. In some cases it ensured the prosperity of the species within hundreds of millions of years (termites, ants), in others this equilibrium was very unstable (most of the marsupials of Australia who disappeared after coming of the Europeans).

The introduced concept of the evolutionary stages shows a quantitative uneven distinction of Man from the animal world. The term an "intellectual animal" applicable to the most representatives of mankind, turns to be incompetent. The behavior of the ant if you take a detached view looks intelligent, but numerous experiments showed that it is rather a biological automaton performing a function strictly specified by the Collective Consciousness.

I AND WE

I tell you this – when started from the Goal,
Over the flaming shoulders of the Foal
Of Heav'n Parwin and Mushtari they flung,
In my predestin'd Plot of Dust and Soul.

Omar Khayyam   (1048-1131)

So, what determines the Line of Destiny, the chain of accidental or, as it seems to us, not accidental events? Why does good luck save and care for and guides from situation to situation somebody but punishes somebody else? Are we really punished? It may be ourselves who arrange all that happens to us, while the outer forces just provide the conditions to implement it. With time course each person performs gradual transition from the outer world to the inner one. The velocity of the inner time changes. The orientation of the whole life cycle changes, as well.

A child is fully dependent on the people who surround it. Without them it is not able to become human; it can not become human without its parents, without their constant understanding care and nourishment. However this is not just physical food. Many examples are known when children were raised by animals: apes, wolves, goats. When they got into the human society they were not people, they were little apes, wolves or goats. All attempts to turn them into people failed. For the development of a baby or a growing teenager of most importance is the information he gets from other people and from the surrounding world. Childhood and youth is the time of communication and socializing, the time of learning the world through other people.

The person more and more immerses into his own concerns. He is more and more focused on his own world and gradually other people surrounding him cease to play a significant role. Finally, he comes alone to the last meeting. At this meeting nobody plays any role, and nobody has any effect on him.

So, what is the relationship of the individual and collective in man? Does the collective consciousness first mentioned by the great psychiatrist-intuit Jung and more and more often used in modern concepts exist? What is it? Is it just an ideal concept, or is there some physical reality behind it? Is it material or ideal? And what is more important in our life, material or ideal?

Looking retrospectively at the chain of the events of my own life, studying history, let it be distorted, known from chronicles, I more and more often come to an idea that all historical events are materialistic realization of the spiral of the development of human spirit. History is governed not by material stimuli, not by ambitions of individual rulers and not by religious confessions. It is advanced by spiritual impulses. And like in many aspects of our life, these impulses are a non-linear sum of inner tensions and outer forces. They are made up of tensions and contradictions that have always existed in human society, and of influences of outer, natural and cosmic factors. In many aspects history is guided by individual and collective spiritual impulses, spiritual urges.

To make this thought clearer and to illustrate it both by the development of individual lives and by collective processes, we need to consider the general model of man that we have been following in recent years. This model shows that man is a unity of three principles, the unity indivisible and unconditional.

One of his parts is physical. It is the physical body, physical processes, all that connects us with the material world, the animal world from which this body originated and to which it belongs in many aspects. Our potencies, desires, connected with satisfaction of material needs, sexual need, all these belong to the material body. They are born by nature, belong to nature and will return into the world of nature after the master's death. The next part of the integer essence of man is spiritual entity. It is the soul, it is the information field, it is an ideal non-materialistic part that exists in the unity with the physical body bur can separate from it and exist as an individual entity. Numerous descriptions of separation of the soul from body after clinical death are known when the person could see his body and the doctors fussing over it. In USA I happened to visit the Monroe Institute whose founder was able to "travel" out of his body, moving in time and space, visiting friends and family. Later on he founded the institute and taught this out of body experience. Well, look around, probably at this very moment you are surrounded by ghosts flying in the air and watching you with interest. I am kidding. However, who knows? Our soul is the medium of our feelings and emotions. This is everything that accumulates ideal strivings, feelings, desires that are not directly associated with the provision of our life processes. The soul is the link of body and spirit, the third component of the entity; the spirit realized in the world entity, cosmic substance, God, the only one for the whole mankind but having many (though countable) modalities.

These three entities, the material body, soul and spirit make up man. The lost of any of them leads to the loss of life. When a person loses his soul he turns into an animal. When he loses a link with the spirit he turns into an automaton. It does not mean that the person must be religious and attend all church services. There are lots of spiritual atheists and soulless church-goers. A link with the spirit is first and foremost the direction aimed at high ideals, devotion to the objectives that are beyond the limits of common vitality; even if most of time the person is focused on it. But if at some moment the person can go to a balcony and admire the sunset getting stunned by its beauty, the beauty of God's creation, his soul absorbs a particle of the universal Spirit.

The main idea that we develop in our studies is that the development of a single man and the whole mankind is first of all the development of the soul, the development of the individual spiritual needs and their satisfaction. The whole man's life is aimed at the satisfaction of the demands of the three entities: physical, soul and spiritual, the essence of the spirit.

It is impossible to live without normal conditions for the material body. If a person is hungry he will first of all think about how to feed his physical body. If he is sexually anxious, the hormones flowing in his body will unconsciously determine all his thoughts and actions. This is the first basic level, without satisfying it you are not able to satisfy the rest.

The first millennia of mankind passed primarily in search of better ways of satisfying this very level. But gradually, after getting more and more products and satisfying physical needs the attention was switched to the soul level. People started to seek the ways to make the soul happy. This formed the grounds for the power of church. This gave start to the birth of music and arts. This led to the greatest importance of beauty in the life of man, and people were ready to pay more and more for beauty, for a sweet song, for a beautiful view from the window. All talks about adornments, beautiful clothes and other things serving for sexual attraction of each other are materialistic nonsense. Men and women have always loved each other, it is one of the most important life stimuli, and the use of adornments and attractive attributes is actually not so important. Rings on fingers and ear-rings first of all bring happiness to their owner and show his belonging to some social group. At any age people get attached to beautiful toys, and adults, compared to children, have more expensive toys. We are drawn to things and phenomena that make our soul happy. And the more an individual soul develops during centuries, the finer, more exquisite joy it requires. Looking at the history of mankind, we will see that it develops in cycles and, at the same time progressively, regularly repeating the same but at a higher level, by a spiral, and each new turn produces more perfect ways of satisfying spiritual demands of man. The history of mankind is the history of human spirit.

An eminent Soviet historian and geographer Lev Gumilev developed his concept of history. He wondered why people living a quiet, inconspicuous to anybody life suddenly rise in unison to form invincible armies and conquer vast territories, create powerful states, and after a few centuries scatter in space and time, leaving only a memory in the annals and legends. Vandals and Goths, Genghis Khan and Timur, the invincible Ottoman warriors are now but only memories. Why do some states dominate for some time, and then again go into oblivion? Lev Gumilev developed a concept that enables us to explain these processes. His concept is based on the idea that at some point of time some external momentum gives to people living in a certain area an extraordinary activity and powerful inspiration. This impulse excites in people their inner energy, "passionarity", as Gumilev called it. Passionarity is energy of the soul giving a strong impetus to the individual development and individual pursuit. Passionary people can not be quiet. They can not live a monotonous daily life, they want adventures; they want action, accomplishment. For them an approval of the companions is much more important than the individual wealth or personal achievements. They do not care about their own lives, or about their own prosperity and well-being. A spiritual idea is what motivates these people. It was so during the times of Genghis Khan who managed to create a myriad army by the spiritual idea for the fight against the Chinese invaders. It was so during the time of the first Christians who endured tremendous persecution and suffering for the sake of a spiritual idea. It was so in all great wars when armies fought driven forward by a spiritual idea.

However, these ideas do not always lead to humanistic manifestations. Wasn't it a spiritual idea that moved the troops of furious Hitler, the idea of creating a new race, a new community of people, the true Aryans, the only descendants of the great tribe? Wasn't it a spiritual idea that enabled the Russian people and their allies to win that war, to overcome the trained, wonderfully equipped Nazi army? Wasn't it a spiritual idea that helped people to survive in unimaginable conditions of the concentration camps: Nazi, Soviet, Korean, and Chinese?

For me a story of my father's life has always been a vivid example. It was a hard and complicated life. The life illuminated by a great spiritual idea. He lived not too long, 70 years, and died during a long trip from an inner overstrain. At the end of his life he wrote memoirs. These pages, written in his hand are part of the history of XX century. They are part of the precious grains of life which disappear often leaving no trace. And the new generation not knowing about these grains, knowing nothing about this experience, repeat the same mistakes and run up against the same rusty nails.

My parents lived a very difficult life, like most of their generation: my mother graduated from the Leningrad Medical Institute in the summer of 1941, and she was sent to work in one of the hospitals. She worked as a doctor in Leningrad during the Siege, and every day walked half the town to bring some food to her father. He survived only because of her care. My father worked as Head of department at Tupolev Aviation Factory in 1938. In autumn 1938 he was arrested and exiled to Siberian prison camps. Through his engineering talent he managed to survive in subhuman conditions, and in 1941 was moved to Moscow to the "engineering sharaga", the prison where designers and engineers under supervision of Tupolev worked to develop new aircraft. There he worked until his release in 1944 for the creation of new types of military aircraft. However, my father was rehabilitated only in 1954, after Stalin's death, and never again he was allowed to work in the aviation industry. Until the end of his life he worked to develop machines for concentration of coal, although his love was aviation.

My father's entire life was under the Soviet power, and his entire life he was a true devotee of the Soviet Communists. When I asked him,

"How can it be so? You went through Stalin's camps, you suffered so much!! For many years you were subjected to bullying and harassment. And now how can you say that the Communist idea is correct?"

He always answered, "Yes. Because those were individual errors of individuals but the very idea of communism is the most right!!!"

Remember the saying? "Those who have not suffered from communism in their youth, have no heart; those who are keen on this idea in adulthood, have no mind". It is easy to say so looking back from XXI century when we can compare the East and West Germany, the North and South Korea, Cuba and Mexico. When we see that the issue is not about good and bad leaders. The issue is in the idea itself! The idea that is fundamentally flawed; the idea, which placed the collective over the personal, which allowed the collective to suppress the personal, to usurp it, to drive into the framework of the ants' order, and, bringing it to a high degree of perfection, led to the complete collapse. XX century is the century of historical lessons. History seemed to put the experiments, purposefully, demonstrating to mankind what is good and what is bad. A democratic society is a society of individual empowerment and collective control. A fascist and communist society is a society of individual repression and totalitarian control. Can we remember these lessons and never repeat such experiments?!

Apparently, early XX century was the time of powerful passionary effects throughout the European world. In the middle of XX century there was a lull, when the processes taking place in the world were listless and protracted. And people with high passionarity and increased energy were mainly focused on individual accomplishments. That is why it was the time of scientific discoveries, designs, the time of writers, artists and armchair scientists. By the end of the century, the intensity of the process again began to increase. The first tremors began in the 70-ies; they caused the strain of the 80-ies and the rapid explosion of the 90-ies. The energy of the Universe began to grow rapidly, increasing passionarity in sensitive individuals and exacerbating chronic illnesses. Humanity was approaching a new phase in its development.

155

STRUCTURE SYNCHRONIZATION
IN A GROUP OF ORGANISMS

Strong reasons make strong actions.

Shakespeare. King John. 3. 4.

It is obvious from the idea about the collective consciousness that a society can be a single organism only if it consists of a certain number of members. We know about peoples and tribes that were completely destroyed and remained only in vague legends. In scientific terms this idea can be formulated in a different way: abolition of a certain number of elements of the system does not affect its functioning until the information signals of the remaining elements in the system are sufficient for resonance synchronization of all elements in the system, i.e., for maintaining the existing structure. When this condition is violated, a more or less strong distortion of the spatial-field structure occurs which leads to distortion of the information signals of the upper level with regard to the lower one, and, respectively, to dysfunction of the weakest elements of the lower level. An important consequence is the concept of the "creative critical mass" we introduce here. It means that the generation of a creative activity can occur only if there is a certain quantity of population in the given place that forms its own structure and, accordingly, its information matrix. A creative activity in this case appears as generation of certain ideas, interaction of these ideas with the information matrix, their enhancement and repeated reflection to their source (but also to other individuals and groups of people).This explains a simultaneous production of the same ideas of different researchers repeatedly observed in the history of science, often in different parts of the globe. A profound need of cities and their role as cultural and scientific centers is also becoming clear. In cities the tension of the information field is particularly high and it affects the intellectual activities of people being in this field. The same process limits the development of peoples living as family groups: in the course of existence, they do not form large and stable enough groups to produce a complex field of consciousness.

A natural objection arises: what about hermits, why great thinkers always left large cities to formulate great ideas? The answer to this question organically follows from the hypothesis. The field of the collective consciousness, structuring and strengthening the new ideas, at the same time imposes its limitations. New ideas become part and development of the existing ones, i.e., part of the existing paradigm formed at this level of structuring. If a man feels the approach of a new idea, i.e., feels the possibility of contact with a field of consciousness of another level of structure, he should maximally get free from the influence of the field of this level for verbal formulation of his ideas. But further development of these ideas and their structuring of the field of consciousness are only possible in a large group. Moses, Buddha, Christ went into the desert for solitude and reflection, but then they returned to people and preached their ideas among many tribesmen. And the ideas of each of them, for all their revolutionary spirit, were presented in the usual form, were associated with the previous paradigm, and at first glance seemed to be its development. Therefore, they got the expansion and propagation. Otherwise, the ideas died, even if they were implemented on the highest level, as it happened with the idea of the single god Pharaoh Akhenaton or with the idea of the aircraft by Leonardo da Vinci.

In terms of the proposed model, the raison d'être of every individual becomes clear, the question that has troubled philosophers for centuries and that occurs before most people by the end of their life. Every single person is an elementary cell, a primary source of information of the field structure of his nation, and then of all mankind. Without these basic cells the emergence and existence of the structure is not possible, with the destruction of a "critical mass of cells" the structure is destroyed. You can draw an analogy with red blood cells: their change within a small range does not affect the state of the body, but beyond these boundaries pathological processes begin. So every single person can be proud that by the only fact of his existence he contributes to the existence and development of mankind.

Another thing is that man through his creative activity can contribute to the global information field. The carefully developed and nurtured ideas, under certain conditions, can form stable images-phantoms that start living independently of their creator. Ideas float about in the air; the same inventions and discoveries are made independently in different parts of the globe. We can give many examples, the most significant of which is the development of spiritual ideas of Mankind.

It is necessary to emphasize the complexity which we attach to the notion of the information field. It includes not only the field structure of the information form-images, but also the ordinary, familiar to us forms of information and communication. Let us represent this as a table, although from the principles outlined above we understand the conventionality and artificiality of such structuring.

Spatial field form-images;

Global communication networks;

TV networks;

Radio broadcasting networks;

Newspapers;

Books;

Special professional documents;

Computer programs including games;

Movies and videos;

Oral communication;

Private correspondence.

One might propose another principle of classification, e.g., by the type of transmitted information, but in this context it is not fundamental, and the main thing is to understand the idea of the significance of each form and their mutual influences.

At this stage of reasoning a significant difference between the developed views and the ideas of the morphogenetic field of Rupert Sheldrake becomes apparent. In our opinion, structural fields of each biological species including Information Fields emerge due to the activity of these species and develop through evolution, together with the development of the species. Therefore, the Darwinian theory of evolution remains fully in force, just as the theory of genetic transmission of hereditary traits. Another additional formative element is introduced into consideration: the structural field of a species formed by the species and evolving along with its development. This eliminates the need for introducing the primary original forms. The evolution of the biological world goes gradually, by an increasingly complex spiral, with transfer of traits from one generation to another, from one species to another, more perfect one. There is no need to use the hypothesis of the Divine impulse, or Space Aliens.

Another point is that all development of life on Earth takes place in the conditions of cosmic influence, and is structured by cosmic matrices. It is difficult to say how formative this influence is and to what extent it determined the specific forms of life on Earth. It may be possible that such a pervasive matrix was cosmic microwave background radiation, which arose at the time of "separation" of radiation from matter, approximately 300,000 years after the birth of the universe [Prigogine, 1994].

The existence of the CMB was predicted in 1948 by Alfred and Herman and experimentally confirmed in 1965 by Penzias and Wilson. This was a truly remarkable discovery that determined the development of modern cosmological ideas. The CMB has a surprisingly high isotropy, permitting its use as a distinguished reference system. With respect to this radiation as a kind of the "new ether", it became possible to measure the direction and speed of the Earth, the Solar system and our Galaxy.

Cosmic microwave background radiation is endowed with yet another exceptional property: its spectrum coincides exactly with the blackbody radiation spectrum (the so-called Planck distribution).This is because in the early stages of the universe there was a complete thermodynamic equilibrium between matter and radiation, resulting in obtaining this spectrum by radiation. As the universe expanded, its temperatures decreased, and the radiation wavelength increased proportionally, but the nature of the spectrum remained unchanged. So it was before the separation of radiation from matter and afterwards, when cosmic radiation experienced the last scattering on matter; the Universe became transparent, and nothing had any effect on its spectral composition. By to date, the peak of spectral distribution of background radiation has reached the millimeter range, which corresponds to temperatures between 2 and 7 ° K. Background radiation reaches the Earth's surface, but the high frequency portion of the spectrum is strongly absorbed by the atmosphere. During the existence of the atmosphere and organic life on Earth there happened no significant shifts of the peak of spectral distribution of the cosmic microwave background radiation.

Measured by A.V. Leontovich, the average length of the natural oscillations of the neuron as an electromagnetic vibrator is 1 cm, which is near the peak in the low-frequency spectrum of the CMB. Thus, the CMB may resonate with neurons. In addition, there is the known and widely used in modern medicine effect of the weak (informational) impact on the acupuncture points with electromagnetic waves of millimeter range, which, as we have seen, coincides with the wavelength of the background radiation near the peak of its spectral distribution. In this connection, it can be assumed that the function of the CMB as a super-stable space system is "tuning" of organic life with the low-frequency part of its spectrum. As for the high-frequency spectrum of the cosmic microwave background radiation, it seems to have no direct effect on organic life, or the effect is much weaker and influences the arrangement of processes of higher levels. By the way, the absorption of this part of spectrum decreases in the mountains, and perhaps that is why it is considered auspicious to "communicate" with the cosmos there. People resonate with the cosmos at "bass notes" but the higher planes of its system respond to the "high notes".

THE INEVITABILITY OF ORDER

> *Had I been present at the Creation,*
> *I would have given some useful hints*
> *for the better ordering of the universe.*
>
> *Alfonso, King of Castile (1221-1284)*

From school years we have lived in the belief that the world is ruled by Chaos, that all creation tends to destruction and any process being on its own can only disorganize. Life is a progress to death. Chaos and Heat Death is an inevitable final of any events. This is the consequence of the Second Law of Thermodynamics, the law, considered as indispensable in physics as the law of conservation of energy. A manifestation of this law is growth of entropy in any process. In accordance with classical concepts, entropy can only increase, which is equivalent to destruction of any ordered structures and their transition to a chaotic state. The end of everything is a homogeneous gas uniformly filling the entire space. This is the consequence of one of the laws of classical physics.

But for some reason this does not happen. We see the world around us, the world existing for billions of years (as far as we know this), that is not going to transform into a uniform chaotic state. On the contrary, this world is getting more complicated; there are roads, houses, computers in it, and this is also part of the global process of the development of nature, the process going under the influence of human consciousness. Everything in the world is following the way of structuring and complexity, and the local chaos, emerging thanks to human activity, is overcome with time and replaced by the order, sometimes under the influence of people, sometimes thanks to the forces of nature. An abandoned house collapses and dies, but after a while in its place a new, improved structure, or a house is built; or, this house is absorbed by vegetation, and becomes a refuge for hundreds of insects and dozens of forest dwellers. The world around us is ordered, structured, and in a constant process of self-organization. It is a law of nature which is much stronger than the second law of thermodynamics.

These ideas, for all their strangeness, are not new. Since the beginning of XX century many thinkers have tried to overcome the limitations of the second law. Schroedinger first managed to do it without breaking the building of classical physics. He introduced the concept of an "open system" and postulated that a decrease in entropy in one point is inevitably associated with an increase in another. This idea made it possible to free us from the ghost of the Heat Death and to send all the "extra" entropy somewhere to the depths of Space. A Nobel Laureate I. Prigogine and H. Haken developed this idea by introducing the concept of synergetic self-organization.

Much more radical was a Belarussian physicist V.I. Veinik who completely rejected the Second law of thermodynamics, and offered his own conception of thermodynamic processes logically explaining the inevitable self-organization of all running processes. The concept of V.I. Veinik was furiously resisted by Soviet physicists, his book was withdrawn from stores and burned (at least not publicly), and he was ostracized till the end of life. Naturally, except a small circle of his adherents, no one learned about his concepts.

We do not intend to engage in deep discussion of conceptual issues on these pages. One thing is important: the world around us does not aspire to chaos and disintegration, on the contrary, it structures and complicates, and life is the highest form of self-organization process. But the foundation of this process is laid on the molecular and quantum levels.

Water is one of the best examples of self-organizing processes. It shows us that order is always more advantageous than chaos.

The enigma of clouds

I'm flying by plane from Minneapolis to New York. Below is a continuous blanket of white clouds. They lie like a white expanse dividing the horizon line with a smooth boundary. There is the sun and blue sky from above and twilight and drizzling rain below. All this would seem to be logically explained by classical physics, by differences in temperature and air pressure.

But what is amazing – the hanging mist is suddenly replaced by grandiose cloud structures. They are piling up in the sky in the form of towers, of bizarre castles, huge domes piled up on each other. These structures are hanging in the sky completely separated from the surrounding space, lonely and still in their grandeur. It seems that you can enter these heavenly palaces and be surrounded by beautiful snow-white robes of the angels in the flying robes.

Obviously, these clouds are complex ordered structures. They are somehow formed from the condensed steam and for a long time retain their shape. It is a vivid example of transition from chaos to an orderly state. If this transition takes place, then it is energetically favorable.

Now let us remember that transition of water into an increasingly ordered state does not require to add energy, but to take it away. To condense vapor into liquid it needs to be chilled; liquid turns into ice when temperature is lowered, then the ordered state under certain conditions appears to be more energetically favorable than chaotic. But for transition into a less ordered state, from ice to liquid, from liquid to vapor, you need to use energy.

Consequently, for the condensed vapor, clouds, the formation of structures is favorable; hard water advantageously takes the form of a perfect crystal, and the ordering process occurs as soon as the optimal conditions are formed.

The Law of Structuring of Nature

Similar processes should be typical for liquid water. From the above arguments it follows that ordered structures should be formed in water, and the state of ordering is energetically more favorable than a homogeneous molecular suspension.

We can talk about the existence of the Law of Structuring Nature which can be summarized as follows: in all processes of nature there is a transition from simpler to more complex structures self-organizing on their own level of complexity in accordance with the principle of minimizing the energy consumption under the given conditions of the environment.

More complex structural and organizational forms require less energy expenditure for their functioning; they are energetically more beneficial than simple forms and are better adapted to change in the parameters of the rounding off environment. Thus, evolution, transition from simpler forms of life to more complex is the consequence of the Law of Structuring.

The Second Law of Thermodynamics is true only for closed systems where there is no energy and information exchange with the environment. For open systems this law does not apply, it is replaced by the Law of Structuring.

An increase of complexity is an inevitable process of development of any system. On Earth this development can be seen as a transition from simpler to more complex forms of existence of matter. In a simplified form this process can be described as follows:

Geological forms → water → organic molecules → simplest biological species → plants → marine organisms → terrestrial organisms→ reptiles → mammals → people → technosphere → cosmosphere.

Thus, man acts as a stage of evolution of Earth participating as a structure-forming element for the next stages of evolution. The development of technosphere from this point of view is a logical step of self-organization in a complex system, the evolutionary process on Earth, and humanity is a "working tool" of Nature.

Moreover, the development of technosphere obeys the basic law of structuring: minimization of the energy consumption.

Indeed, with the improvement of technology, devices consume less energy per unit of work. For example, consider the improving means of transport: horse traction → steam engine → gasoline engine → hybrid engine **>** water engine→ vacuum motor →...

Even more indicative is the development of artificial intelligence: the mechanical counting devices — vacuum tube computers — solid state computers — microelectronic computers — quantum computers whose development goes at an increasing rate and gives us absolutely fantastic prospects.

As it follows from this analysis, the development of technosphere is an indispensable consequence of the law of structuring, and humanity acts as an actuator in the process, an active medium through which the conversion process is realized.

The next stage of evolution is the development of cosmosphere, the active process of mastering the outer space. We can only fantasize where humanity will come to in 2100...

Thus, all the arguments about the impasse of civilization, about the environmental, economic or social crisis are groundless. They are based on analysis of current transient processes without taking into consideration their long-term global dynamics. Local minima are possible, i.e., periods of recession and stagnation, but in general the evolutionary process moves towards sustained development.

Humanity acts as a form-building factor of nature, directed, however, not at transformation of the ecological environment, but at formation of new elements of Nature, techno- and cosmosphere.

Slogans on the conquest of nature turned to be untenable; the uncontrolled economic activity led to a sharp deterioration of ecological environment, and this situation began to improve only in the last quarter of XX century. It is obvious that we can only use natural resources, only to consume, and the attempts to positively transform the environment is still in its infancy state.

The global problem of mankind is the development of evolution by creating technosphere with maximum preservation of the Earth's resources.

CIVILIZATION IS BUT A BRIEF MOMENT IN THE EARTH'S HISTORY. CIVILIZATION IS AN INEVITABLE STAGE OF DEVELOPMENT OF THE UNIVERSE

Human civilization has existed for several thousand years, perhaps tens of thousands of years. In any case, it is certain that 40 thousand years ago, when the Great Glacial Epoch was ending, groups of mammoth hunters clad in animal skins and armed with stone tools roamed through the expanses of the European plain. Of course, we can assume that at the same time, in a warmer climate, the advanced civilization of Atlantis created poetry and paintings. However, no significant signs of civilizations, cities, temples, and works of art had been found before a few thousand years ago. Perhaps there were some splashes of civilization, not known to us, and there are numerous accounts, by crumbs collected by enthusiasts, but they left neither any grandiose ruins, nor traces in the memory of man. So the development of humanity is a brief moment in the history of Earth, the last paragraphs in the Book of Life of our planet.

If we describe the history of Earth in the book each page of which will be devoted to one million years of evolution, this volume will approximately consist of five million pages. Imagine the thickness of this tome. Let us bind the books in volumes of a thousand pages each, and put these five volumes in a series on a shelf. In the last two volumes there will be description of the deployment of life on Earth, and with each page this description will become more and more saturated. The last volume is a fascinating picture of the appearance and disappearance of new types of living creatures, their interpenetration, development, and abrupt transformations. And in the last volume, on the very last page, the last few lines will read: "Homo Sapiens has appeared. The process of civilization transformation has begun. Gradually, this process has begun increasingly to affect the Earth's ecosystem, leading to a gradually increase of its degradation. The human society has become a transforming force of the Noosphere process"...

In the meanwhile this book ends. How it will continue depends on us. On our collective intelligence. Only one thing is clear now, the appearance of you and me, the development of our civilization is no accident, not the result of random mutations under the influence of unpredictable factors but a logical consequence of the development of the Universe. Here are some arguments in favor of this assertion.

In the mid-twentieth century the so-called **Anthropic Principle** gained popularity in cosmology. Its essence can be explained by the assertion that human existence with its specific structure is possible only with choice of well-defined combinations of the fundamental physical constants from an infinite set of possible values. If even one of these variables had been different, the development of organic life in the universe would have been impossible. In other words, the existence of man imposes restrictions on the possible structure of the Universe.

B.D. Carter distinguishes between the strong and weak Anthropic Principle. He formulates the strong principle as follows: "The universe must be such that at some stage of evolution there could be an observer in it".

And this is the weak principle: "What we expect to observe must satisfy the conditions necessary for human presence as an observer".

According to the great humanist ideas of Pierre Teilhard de Chardin, the human being is the most synthetic state of the "tissue of the universum", besides it is the most dynamic and is undergoing constant development. It is possible to learn how the world was formed and what its further fate is only by "decoding" man. For these reasons the future synthetic science will take man as a basis. This will be a new era in science, with complete understanding that man as an object of knowledge is "the key to the whole science about nature".

This idea has been known to mankind since ancient times.

According to ancient Chinese ideas, between the two cosmic forces, Heaven and Earth, there is the third one, Man. The boundaries between the animate and inanimate in the Chinese natural philosophy are effaced. All is spiritualized and full of life; there is no significant difference between the world and man. Man is not opposed to the world, he is a part of it, and ultimately, he is the world himself:

"What fills the Heaven and Earth is my being. What reigns in Heaven and on Earth is my nature. People are my brothers. Things are my companions". Chang Tsai "Se min"

The concepts of recognizing the universal property of animacy of the world are rooted in the ancient animism and characterize in varying degrees all ancient civilizations. The elements of these concepts can be found in the works of the ancient Greek philosophers, Anaximenes, Heraclitus, Plato, etc. The idea of the general animation of the universum is pretty much typical of Egyptian, Babylonian, Indian and Chinese cultures. The ideal sought by the Chinese perfectly-wise was a "natural" person being in harmony with the "humanized world" and following the "live" rhythms of nature. Different structural levels of the cosmos were considered by the ancient as a single organism, whose parts compose a well-coordinated ensemble.

For example, in Plato's "Tim" the cosmos is likened to "a perfect and intelligible living being". The body of this cosmic being "was cleverly arranged so as to receive food from its own corruption, performing all actions and states in itself and through itself".

A holy book of ancient India Rig Veda (X, 90) speaks of a giant cosmic first man Purusha, from whose parts the Universe was formed: the Sun from the eyes, the airspace from the navel, the sky from the head, the land from the feet, etc. With similar views echoes the Chinese myth of Pangu, recorded in III-IV centuries AD.

XX century was marked by a great revolution in physics, the awareness of the limited character of Newton-Cartesian model, a mechanistic approach to the Universe. Surprisingly, but this approach has kept its power when considering the mental processes of the role and location of Consciousness in the world, despite the many facts that point to its limitations. New ideas are forming gradually, accumulating data and ideas, in order that at some point, by an impetus, they will translate the Public Consciousness in a new way of thinking. This point is increasingly approaching. Its approach depends on us.

FROM PARAPSYCHOLOGY TO SCIENCE

It is true, we no longer burn witches, but we burn every letter that contains the truth.

Georg Christoph Lichtenberg (1742-1799)

Perhaps one day the paranormal will be normal or will eventually be rejected as groundless. Be that as it may, the decision should be taken on the basis of sound scientific criteria but the inconvenient paradigm should not be indiscriminately denied.

Paul Davis. "Project of Universe" (2009)

Literature describes thousands of cases of spontaneous mental communication between people, especially between family members in case of danger or in near-death states. Scientific studies of mental data began in the late XIX century, and were particularly active in the XX century. One of the first serious researchers was a French psychologist and Nobel laureate Charles Richet. In 1889 he published a report describing the experiments when the hypnotized person statistically successfully guessed the contents of a sealed opaque envelope. Similar experiments were continued in early XX century but with the participation of people in the normal state of consciousness[3]. In particular, a psychologist John E. Coover from Stanford University in the United States began telepathic tests using ordinary playing cards. The inductor and percipient were in the adjacent rooms. 97 inductors and 105 percipients were tested, over 10000 attempts altogether. The number of correct guesses referred to random as 160:1. Such tests were replicated by several researchers, also with a positive result; but the greatest influence on public opinion was made by the book of Upton Sinclair "Mental Radio" published in 1930. The wife of Mr. Sinclair, Mary, intrigued by telepathy, trained

---

[3] Here and further cited from: Radin D. The Conscious Universe. 1997, Harper Edge, 362 p.

herself in guessing the pictures drawn by her husband or someone else from the family members. Of 290 tests she correctly reproduced 65, which is a significant result, far superior to a random chance. The wonderful words written by a friend of the family, Albert Einstein, after reading the book are:

"I read the book by Upton Sinclair with great interest, and I am convinced that this subject deserves careful consideration, not only from amateurs, but professional psychologists. The results of the telepathic experiments carefully and clearly presented in this book are far superior to the ideas that a researcher of nature considers possible. On the other hand, in case of such sincere observer as Upton Sinclair, there is no doubt in accuracy of his presentation; his faith and reliability cause no doubt".

Experiments with guessing cards were carried out by Professor Joseph Rhine at Duke University in the United States from 1920 to 1965. J. Rhine used 25 special cards with different images, shown to the inductor in random order. The percipient had to guess the card. Using this scheme J. Rhine and his followers on the whole made 3, 6 million attempts involving 4,600 participants; the results were described in 142 articles. The statistical meta-analysis of these data showed that the probability of correct guessing was significantly higher than the random level.

The comparison level is determined by the fact that when guessing playing cards with five symbols the probability of random response was 20%. This figure is obtained by multiple repetitions of the same tests. In various versions of the experiments the obtained figures were slightly above this level, but with a statistically significant level. Thus, when finding guessable cards in an opaque envelope on the basis of 130,000 attempts in the 6 studies the probability of correct guesses was 20, 85% ± 0, 25%; when a card was placed behind an opaque screen in 497,000 attempts in 16 studies it was 21, 75 % ± 0, 1%; during a telepathic transfer of 164,000 attempts in 10 studies 21, 5% ± 0, 25%; when guessing the card, which will be chosen later in 115,000 attempts in 2 studies 20, 6% ± 0, 25%. Variability given for the reliability level was 0, 95.

As it can be seen from these figures, in all schemes of the experiments the probability of correct guessing of cards was significantly higher than the probability of random guessing. A large number of attempts, carried out independently by researchers from different countries within 60 years, convincingly demonstrated the significance of the obtained data. The experiments with cards ensured the ease of evaluation and processing of the results, but they had a fundamental flaw: participants were quickly tired of sorting the cards and the efficiency sharply decreased, often below the random level. Therefore, in XX century researchers began to develop other schemes of experiments.

An interesting field of research was telepathic **experiments in one's sleep.** They were started under the leadership of Montague Ullman and Stanley Krippner in the U.S. in 1966-1972. The inductor sent certain pictures to the sleeping percipient at the time when he entered the active phase of sleep associated with dreaming. The presence of such phase was determined by EEG and eye movements of the percipient. Upon completion of this phase, the latter was awakened and he talked about his dream. This story was recorded and evaluated by an independent expert to determine the presence of the transferred elements.

The probability of accidental coincidence of the elements in one's sleep with the transmitted information is estimated as 50%. On the average, according to experts in different sessions, the probability in a set of elements and their level of coincidence with the transmitted image was from 30 to 100%. The total number of sessions on dreaming was 450. On the whole, in 450 sessions the probability of coincidence was 63% with 4% of variability at the reliability level of 0, 95, and 5% at the reliability level 0, 99. Thus, it is possible with 99% of certainty to say that the average reliability of data transfer in the state of active sleep is about 63%. This is equivalent to guessing a correct card out of 75 million.

The development of the idea of telepathy in the dream became the so-called **"ganzfeld"** *technique,* from a German word that means "out of the field". The idea was that our nervous system and brain work not only as a detector and processor of sensory information, but also as a filter. This filter handles a huge mass of sensory input constantly breaking on us and selects for the consciousness only those signals that may be relevant or important for survival.

For instance, if in a noisy room someone pronounces your name and you hear it, despite the din of voices. Subconscious processes of information processing were studied in psychology, and we know now that only a small portion coming from outside signals reaches consciousness. Most of them are processed, evaluated and filtered.

Therefore, if you create the conditions under which man will be protected from the entry of external information, his system will become much more sensitive to weak effects. Artificial restriction on external signals is called **sensory deprivation**. If a person is isolated from all external sounds, any light sources, and even put into a salt water pool that compensates the gravitational force where he will be suspended as a child in his mother's womb, this can create an environment of a complete sensory deprivation. After a dozen minutes in such situation without any bottom or top, where no information is perceived, the person loses the sense of his body and begins to transform the information coming from the subconsciousness in fantastic images. This state can be achieved through internal mental settings, in everyday life, and the person ceases to perceive the stimuli coming from outside. The external world as if disappears, and only the man himself and his inner world remain. In all techniques of mental training, meditation or deep prayer a modification of sensory deprivation is used.

During the "ganzfeld" experiments the percipient was in a soundproof chamber with steel walls, shielded from outside noise and electromagnetic fields; the entire experiment was computer-controlled to avoid accidents and errors. In addition, two professional conjurers watched the entire course of the experiment and did not find any flaws in it.

From 1947 to 1997, 2549 ganzfeld experiments were conducted and the results were published in 40 papers around the world. In 1985, a statistical meta-analysis of the published by the time data was carried out, which showed $37\% \pm 2\%$ probability of correct definitions at 25% level of random coincidences. Skeptics suggested a number of possible experimental errors that were taken into account in subsequent sessions.

Meta-analysis of data obtained after 1982 showed the probability of 33, 2%, which corresponds to guessing a single event out of 10^9. Similar experiments have continued in the U.S. and Scotland. Their essential feature is a need for expert evaluation of the obtained data;

that is why it is difficult to imagine a possibility of using such procedures for effective transfer of information

Very close to those described are the **experiments on the distant vision** where the percipient tries to visualize a picture of the surrounding terrain or a selected object observed by the inducer.

Attention to such studies was attracted by the artist Ingo Swann, who described many cases of remarkable coincidences of the seen and sent pictures. In 1970, several government organizations in the U.S. launched a work on the study of distant vision which lasted 24 years, cost 20 million and brought some very interesting scientific results, which, however, were found to be utterly useless for practical application.

After evaluation of the results of the long-term experiments, the government commission reached the following conclusions.

1.　　It was found that the so-called free vision with which the operators can describe everything that comes to mind were more successful than an imposed vision, where the operator offers to choose one of several proposed objectives.

2.　　A small group of selected operators showed clearly better results than random operators. This fact is a strong evidence of the reality of distant vision, since otherwise there should not be any difference.

3.　　Mass selection in search of talented operators showed that among a large group of the tested approximately 1% of people showed reproducibly high results.

4.　　Neither practice nor training could significantly affect the ability to distant vision. Apparently, it depends only on the initial faculties.

5.　　It is unclear whether operators need feedback on their performance, but it creates a level of psychological confidence.

6.　　Neither electromagnetic shielding, nor distance to the target can affect the results.

An expert Jessica Utts, Professor of Statistics at the University of California completes her conclusion with the following words,

"It is clear that the anomalous perception is possible and was demonstrated. This conclusion is based not on faith, but on the accepted scientific criteria. The phenomenon was reproduced in several forms in different laboratories and countries.

I think that to gather further evidence is a waste of valuable time and resources. None of the reviewers evaluating the totality of data at different laboratories found any errors in the evaluation of more improvable and correlated data".

Dean Radin[4] presents in his book a comparison of the meta-analysis data for various types of mental telepathy experiments over several decades. As shown, in all cases the results are statistically superior to 50% level of random guessing. All attempts of skeptics to find errors in the formulation or analysis of such experiments were consistently denied. The results were successfully reproduced in thousands of sessions worldwide, and the effectiveness of trained operators was higher than that of random volunteers. It is important to note that the data are averaged over many thousands of attempts, while in separate sessions 100% was achieved not just once. Thus, all the above data show the reality of mental communication, and now the question is about choosing the most suitable for a particular purpose way to organize the experiment.

In some experiments on telepathy we measured **various subconscious physiological reactions**. Interestingly, even among experts there is a little known fact that the electroencephalograph was invented by a German psychiatrist Hans Berger in 1929 to answer the question whether telepathy could be explained by brain waves.

Two types of experiments on mental (or psy) effect on the human body were developed: a study of physiological correlations of **conscious** perception and the use of physiological parameters as detectors of **unconscious** perception. In most experiments the activity of the autonomous or central nervous system of the percipient was recorded, while the inductor tried in one way or another to affect the percipient sending emotions or other relevant information.

In 1963, one of the pioneers of research of consciousness, Charles Tart in the U.S., measured skin conductivity, blood volume, heart

---

[4] Radin D. The Conscious Universe. 1997, Harper Edge, 362 p.

rate, and recorded the statements of the subjects in these experiments. He also was an inductor subjected to electric shock, while members of his laboratory recorded the presence of subconscious reaction to the pain felt by Dr. Charles Tart in the percipients. In many cases a correlation was observed with the time of feeding current and a change in physiological parameters of the "receiver", while in the percipient's consciousness no signals were observed.

Similar studies were caught up by a number of scientists, both in U.S. and Europe, and in 60-70-ies several publications about these studies appeared. In particular, significant changes, were recorded in the blood volume of a finger of the percipient when the inductor sent him emotions from a distance of thousands of kilometers. It is obvious that gas discharge images will also change, which was successfully recorded in a number of experiments. Significant contribution in this area was made by the researchers from U.S, R. Targ and H.E. Puthoff. They conducted a large series of convincing experiments and in 1974-1976, published articles in the prestigious journals "Nature" and "Proceedings of the IEEE". The very fact of these publications proves a high level of organization of work and the importance of the results. In 1979 all three investigators: C.T. Tart, R. Targ and H.E. Puthoff jointly published a very interesting book "Mind at Large" where a detailed analysis of the results and prospects of distant transfer of emotion was given. In 90-ies several articles were published on the recording of brain activity in telepathy. In particular, in a leading journal "Science" there was a study published by physiologists who had found significant correlations between patterns of electroencephalograms of the brain of two identical twins separated from each other.

The most systematic experiments on the distant transmission of information were held by a psychologist William Braud with colleagues, especially with an anthropologist Marilyn Schlitz. These studies, conducted during 17 years in Texas, were focused on recording different physiological reactions of the subject under a remote influence of the inductor. In 1991 a review of all the experiments was made, which included 655 sessions where 153 people were inducers and 449 people or animals were percipients.

37% of the experiments gave statistically significant results with a probability of random coincidence of 109: 1, 57% of the experiments were successful with a probability better than 20:1 and 6% of experiments gave random results. Thus, these results provided convincing evidence of subconscious reaction of the nervous system of humans and animals under a focused remote influence.

The figure shows the results of the meta-analysis of the published data on the measurements of the electrical under-skin resistance under telepathic influence studied by William Braud, Marilyn Schlitz and other researchers. The inductor is given a task either to direct attention to the percipient, or think of something extraneous to the test sessions. In all cases people are at a distance from each other, in the whole series of experiments in shielded and soundproof rooms. Data were brought into accord with the 50% scale of random variations by comparing the values of resistance in the working and control periods. Each session usually consisted of 10-20 periods of 1-minute transmission and intervals of about 20-30 minutes.

The results were quite different from experiment to experiment, as could be expected without special selection of subjects. The cumulative effect of these 400 trials was 53%, well above the random 50%.

W cannon but note a series of experiments conducted in Russia by a physiologist O.I. Koekina. Using electroencephalography she explored the state of the brain electrical activity in people in various states of consciousness. For example, she made a synchronous mapping of electroencephalographic activity of the brain of the inductor and percipient placed in different buildings. When establishing a contact, a strong correlation between the dynamics of change in brain activity was observed that enabled O.I. Koekina to introduce the concept of the "virtual brain"[5]: the brain operating as a single system when the two persons are at a considerable distance from each other. In all these experiments the inducer was a professional healer. In another series of experiments we identified the peculiarities of brain activity during the transition into the Altered State of Consciousness. It was shown that various states of meditation, "floating in space", "out of body experience" are characterized by a specific nature of brain activity, i.e., they are not just a figment.

If a person can influence another person, it is obvious that such effects may be produced on animals, as well. All owners of livestock know that

[5] Koekina O. Virtual Brain. Consciuosness and Physical reality. 1:1. 1996. pp 96-102. . 3:6. 1998. pp 56-63. (in Russian).

their pets, from dogs and cats to turtles and snakes, actively respond to their master's presence. In a scientific experiment this was demonstrated in the beautiful experiments of Professor Speransky in Novosibirsk, who all his life has used mice for laboratory research. He developed an original method of selection of mice by groups, with the same type of behavior and physiology in a group. These groups proved to be very convenient to work off the effects of different drugs. Professor Speransky successfully used this approach for monitoring mental effects. In the experiments the operator is given a picture of a mouse in advance. Mentally tuned to this particular mouse, the operator tries to change its state, say the appetite, moreover, from a distance of dozens of meters to thousands of kilometers, for example, from Moscow to Novosibirsk. In many cases, the effect caused no doubt: the mouse began gaining weight or grew thin, depending on the operator's goals. Note that even for an experienced biologist is not easy to distinguish from a specific group the mouse, for a no-professional it is practically impossible. Based on the experiments, Professor Speransky developed a method for monitoring the efficiency of the operator's activity which is effectively used in his laboratory.

In recent years, the effects of distant influence acquired a new, technological trend. In the laboratories the design of human-thought-electrode-wire device has been implemented. The development team from Fraunhofer Institute for Computer Architecture and the doctors of Charité Berlin Clinic, headed by Professor Dr. Klaus-Robert Müller and Gabriel Curio have developed the system of Brain Computer Interface. They are confident that the thought-controlled computer will give people deprived of the joy of motion a possibility not to lose a touch with the outside world and take care of themselves.

A "cap" with 128 (2^7) electrodes is put on the subject's head; brain signals are deciphered, and volunteers with only mental commands type the specified text. Slowly but correctly. Typing short phrases requires from 5 to 10 minutes. The system learns by itself and identifies the "palettes" of signals for each person individually.

In addition to purely scientific interest, the control over the power of thought is of practical interest to people who can not communicate with others in another manner. Clearly, those are, above all, paralyzed patients. Typing goes on slowly, but for the paralyzed it is great progress, as before that they could communicate with other people by blinking only.

Similar works are carried out in the U.S. and Russia. The development team from the Institute of Higher Nervous Activity and Neurophysiology led by academician Igor Shevelev, Head of the Laboratory of Physiology of Sensory Systems, obtained the same result almost simultaneously with their German colleagues: their subjects can type words of three or four letters using their mental activity. As noted by academician Igor Shevelev, three different processes can be used in such devices. It is the so-called P300 wave, which occurs in the brain when the person sees a stimulus significant for him. For example, the monitor shows a computer keyboard which displays columns one after another. When the one with a conceived a letter lights up, a more prominent wave appears in the brain. A computer program instantly detects and processes it. The Germans use the principle of μ-rhythm, which arises not in the visual but motor centers of the cerebral cortex, when a person is thinking about the necessary movement, for example, about turning an arrow or moving the cursor. And, finally, the so-called adaptive interface can be used, when a man conceives a certain state or image. In Russia all three approaches are investigated.

As we see, telepathy is a real process based on the brain electrical activity. Numerous empirical and experimental data prove that it is a real fact and not such a rarity in our life. Perhaps our ancestors being much more sensitive to subliminal signals could communicate telepathically. We lost that feeling, but imagine what chaos would be in our heads if we continuously received mental images of all the near and far, even if only from friends and relatives. We would have no time to live our own life. So that blocking of telepathy is a certain point of the evolutionary development. Moreover, this feature can be used for practical purposes.

I don't like making phone calls. You may press buttons for a long time, and the other end is busy or does not answer. That is why I mastered the technique of "call back". When I need to connect with some friend, I mentally send him a request to call me, and after a while, as a rule, the bell rings. You need just to tune in on the person: imagine him and politely ask to call you. Try it and see what you get.

TELEPATHY

> *Welcome to Telepathics Anonymous.*
> *Don't bother introducing yourself.*
>
> *Benson Bruno, Evergreens Are Prudish*

The mid-eighties are called the time of "stagnation". The aged Brezhnev could no longer control the situation in the country, but any government official was trying to keep the situation unchanged by all means. Officials and elders are afraid of changes. Everyone realized that something had to be changed, but no one dared to undertake it. A group of elderly politicians headed by Brezhnev and the KGB chief Andropov tenaciously held the mechanisms of power and the power apparatus. The system created by Stalin was so stable that nearly 40 years outlived its creator. The rarest event in the history of dictatorships!

However, it was not the worst of times for the Soviet science. The rulers of all countries made certain of the practical power of science and began to respect its employees. It turned out that the most extravagant of scientists such as Einstein and Bohr, sometimes gave birth to very practical ideas. Thus their extravagance had to be endured and their ideas listened to, even if they seemed crazy. Especially if those ideas promised some prospects for the military industry. In this case no money was spared.

That is why in the eighties in different countries the projects on military use of human psychic energy were initiated. As fate willed it, I was involved in one of such projects.

The task was purely practical: to create a telepathic communication with submarines. Radio communication with boats located at a depth is a very difficult task. The problem is that radio waves almost do not penetrate into the salty water. So the boats had to float in order to communicate with the authorities. Obviously, communication required new physical principles. It was then that someone from the big bosses read popular books about paranormal abilities and came across a chapter on telepathy and found that it had long and unsuccessfully practiced in the world. After a series of high-level meetings it was decided to organize a lab and charge it to develop a system of telepathic communication within three years.

It happened just by accident: during an outing I met a friend who, as it turned out, was in charge of establishing that laboratory. We had not seen for five years. After an exchange of platitudes, he suddenly asked,

"I've heard you're studying the Kirlian effect. Is it true that this method can record psycho-emotional states?"

"Of course, this is one of the main advantages of the method", I replied.

A week later (apparently after a careful check on my reliability), I was offered the post of a deputy head of the lab with good salary.

This is how the chance meeting led to another bout of fate. Many things have their own hidden laws. It is remarkable that the meeting was in the same suburb Solnechnoe near Petersburg, where once I had so 'successfully" jumped from the roof. I came to this village for the first time after many years... Our working conditions were actually perfect. The funds were virtually unlimited. We had only to make advance estimates. We were provided with any equipment at our discretion. The era of personal computers had just begun, but our team of programmers received all the latest novelties. Of course, now they seem like children's toys.

But most remarkable was that we were given free rein. We could do what we considered necessary and only occasionally were to report on the results. But that was obligatory.

None of the world's developed methods of mental sending of information provided reliable data transmission. And this is one of the main requirements for practical applications. From the viewpoint of information theory, any communication channel consists of the three main elements:

A transmitted message is encoded and supplied to the transmitter; then it is transmitted to the receiver through the communication line, after which decoding takes place. For example, in the TV channel the visual information is encoded in a TV-signal, analog or digital; it is radiated by the transmitter in the form of radio waves, arrives at the receiver tuned to this wave, and is decoded into an image in the television set.

In the case of a telepathic communication channel, the transmitter and receiver were people; we could only speculate about the communication line, but the process of encoding and decoding needed to be considered. What to take? Zener Cards? Pictures? Emotional images of views of a calm sea and horrors of the war?

After several weeks of reflections and debates someone suddenly remembered healers. What are they doing in the course of treatment?

•   Affect other people.

•   Can we measure the time of impact?

We began to look through books and journals. With some difficulty we found a couple of articles about exotic measurements of electroencephalograms (EEG) of patients during healing sessions. Significant changes were observed.

•   What about hypnosis? It is also a very close process.

Again we carried out directory search. The catch was meager, but hopeful. It became obvious that in the process of mental impact a change in the electrical brain signals is observed.

•   What happens to the Kirlian glow? Will it change?

As it turned out, nobody knew, but it was worth trying. Thus the experimental scheme was born. The signal is given to the transmitter-inductor (a flashing lamp), and he sends the effect to the receiver-percipient. The latter is sitting in the lab, in another room, and his EEG and Kirlian glow are constantly measured. At the first step it was necessary to verify whether changes of electric signals synchronized with the flashing lights of the inductor will occur.

Another question: whether to take for the experiments random people, as Americans do, or specifically selected? Here the opinion was unanimous: it is necessary to prepare specially selected pairs. The practice of healing has shown: there are talents, and there are masters and apprentices. You can teach anyone to feel energy, but to really work effectively a talent from God is required.

We contacted a colleague who led a large center for mental abilities training, and within a few days the experiment began.

Surprisingly, the result was obtained in the first experiment. The healer, a nice man of 40, brought a patient, a pretty young woman. We explained the objectives of the work, showed the equipment, and they gladly agreed to participate in the experiments. They were interested to see what would happen if we recorded something.

Generally, it should be noted that working with traditional healers and psychics is very nice. As a rule, they enjoy the experiment and participate in discussions with interest. Although, as with any group of people, among them there is a variety of psychological types, and sometimes working with them requires a special approach. But I will talk more about that later, in the following chapters.

Thus, the inductor and percipient were in different rooms with wires on them, and after 15 minutes of relaxation exercises the inductor was given the sign: "Here we go!" The percipient was in a relaxed state but awake. We did not use the technique of dreams, although it is also very interesting and promising. The lamp flashes and the face of the inductor looks focused and detached. A minute later he looks visibly relieved. Again there comes a flash, then a break. With time we learned to transmit this way the Morse code signals, i.e., whole phrases and messages. After the experiment the data taken from the percipient are processed, and the points of signal changes are detected by the EEG and Kirlian. These points are marked on the time axis and compared with the timing lights. Victory! Almost 70% of the significant coincidence! The communication channel works! (Fig.32)

Communication channel

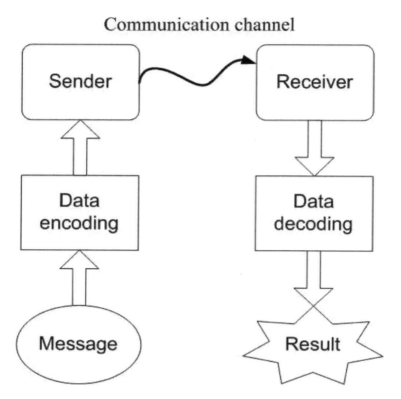

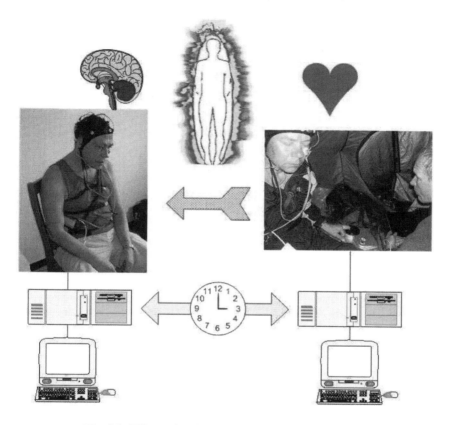

Fig.32. The principle of telepathy experiments

It took almost a year to refine the details of the experiments. We checked several dozen pairs, and revealed an interesting pattern: even with the best of them the work efficiency decreased as the experiments were carried on. It was the highest in the first-second session, and then decreased, reaching a stable level for the fifth-sixth experiment, and remained at that level thereafter. Simultaneously with a decrease in the efficiency of the directed transmission or directed effect, the frequency of spontaneous, non-programmable telepathic communication between members of the pair increased. People felt the moment when they needed to call each other, they saw the same dreams, independently and simultaneously bought the same things, magazines, products, they were simultaneously sad or happy. And it depended neither on age or sex of the pair members. The only requirement was mutual sympathy

A year later, we were able to report 85% efficiency of the telepathic communication channel. The system worked. There are methods for selecting and training participants of the experiment; the conditions for a transition into an altered state of consciousness necessary for efficient operation of the inductor were worked out. Naturally, we also went through all training and after a while conducted a telepathic communication in daily practice. Of course, it was on a fairly simple level. Until now, when I need to connect with some person and the situation can wait for a few days, I concentrate on his image and ask him to contact me. After some time the telephone rings or, even more strangely, I meet this man on the street or in the metro. It is a very handy feature: it saves a lot of time and money, especially for international calls.

After many years the life spiral made another turn and I was again involved in a study of telepathy. It happened during our expeditions to the Himalayas, to the foot of Mount Everest, to the jungles of Venezuela and valleys of Peru, from where our Moscow colleagues organized sessions of mental communication with Moscow, and we measured their energy and information state with our techniques (Fig. 33). But that's another story.

By the way, in the eighties we came to the conclusion that telepathy is absolutely not suitable for communication with submarines. 85% efficiency would be quite acceptable. The reliability of communication by paralleling channels can always be improved. But the human factor plays a very important role in this process. This is the percipient factor.

In the process of telepathic communication one participant was active: he trained and worked actively changed his state; the second one was in peaceful relaxation. As it turned out, it was not easy to maintain this state doing nothing for a long period of time. After some time, the person just got bored. He either started to fall asleep during the experiments, or lost sensitivity, thinking about something else. For military purposes it was no good. We had to find some solutions, or to end the program. Nobody wanted that, as everything was very interesting and exciting.

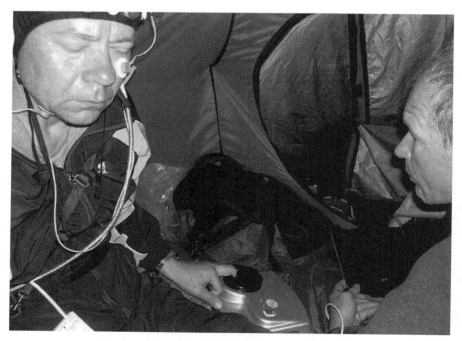

Fig.33. Pictures from telepathy experiments

SENSORS

*Why, sir, there is every possibility
that you will soon be able to tax it!*

*(to Gladstone, when asked about
the usefulness of electricity).*

Michael Faraday ((1791-1867)

At some point, we unanimously came to the conclusion that we
needed to work out the impact of humans on physical sensors. To
keep the percipient on a submarine for months is a costly and
thankless task. However if we could put a sensor responding to mental
impact, the communication channel could become practically useful. I
immediately thought of our experiments with Vadim Polyakov and
made drawings of the sensor. A month later the pilot plant was ready.

By that time we had accumulated some experience working with
psychics and understood that the work required special conditions. In
town, when a person comes to experiments for a few ours, tearing
himself away from other things, he needs a certain time to tune in, to
feel aloof from current affairs and concerns and to enter an altered
state of consciousness. Afterwards this state can be maintained for a
long time, but the working day quickly comes to an end, and the
experiments are also necessary to be finished. It was therefore
decided to organize a summer visiting session. As I mentioned earlier,
money in those days was not considered. We submitted the
substantiation of the study, explained all to our authorities, and after a
while were looking for a summer retreat. After going through several
options, we chose the building of a medical college in one of the
Baltic republics. There were no classes held in summer, and we
rented the building for two months. The conditions were perfect: a
small Baltic town that had preserved the national identity and charm
for over 40 years of the Soviet occupation; cozy houses with tiled
roofs, a Polish Roman-Catholic church, saved from being ruined by
the heroic efforts of local patriots, a huge shady park. By that time the
residents of the Baltic republics had already submitted to their
position as part of the Soviet empire, the attitude to the Russians was
friendly, and only at a close acquaintance and intimate conversations

one could feel a hidden hatred to the country-occupier. In the eighties we felt in the Baltic republics cozy and comfortable.

We brought the equipment, and a week later everything was ready for work. Part of the rooms was reserved for the work and part for living. The house stood in the middle of the park, surrounded by high oaks, and our activities did not attract anybody's attention.

According to the results carried out within a year of experiments, we selected a group of talented psychics, and they stayed two weeks living and working in the summer retreat, leaving it just to walk along the alleys of the park or go to the nearest store. After a couple of days, people forgot about their affairs and concerns, and fully immersed in an atmosphere of meditation, measurements, and leisurely evening conversations. For enthusiasts there was an opportunity to visit the parties at a nearby leisure spa where groups of bored young girls and women were happy not to resist the persistent attacks of the young scientists. The head of Laboratory looked at the adventures through his fingers and periodically stayed in rooms of pretty girls-strangers. The only requirement was to be at the workplace at 9 a.m. Fortunately, we could always sleep after lunch.

And here is the first experimental day. The equipment has been checked; the sensor is turned on and tuned to. A few people have gathered in the laboratory room, including the chief of the laboratory and one of our powerful psychic-operators, Leonid, proven in healing and telepathic sessions. I feel extremely uncomfortable: what if all this is in vain? What if nothing will work? May it be just by accident with Polyakov? On the oscilloscope screen there is a flat trembling string of pulses. This is the background. In this state the sensor can remain for many hours, and the signal is almost constant, with slight variations. I explain the task to Leonid: to influence the sensor in this metal box. He asks,

"What kind of influence should it be? What to transfer: feelings, teams, emotions?"

How do I know? As a joke I answer,

"Try to love it. Imagine that in this cell there is a pretty young princess, and you are her Prince-rescuer".

Leonid focuses. His face takes an aloof, thoughtful look, his eyes become glassy and plunges inside. A minute passes, then two minutes, five minutes. A series of pulses is on the screen as if nothing has happened. I understand that nothing has come of it and try not to look at anybody. Once again I glance at the screen. It's time to stop. Why to fool the people... And suddenly I see the pulses on the oscilloscope screen begin to grow in size and seem to expand. What is it? Hallucinations? But no, a string of pulses is actively creeping up. The recorder that was quietly drawing a straight line some time before becomes choppy and confidently deflects aside.

"We've got it", says the head of the laboratory with confidence. The silence in the lab is suddenly broken; everyone starts moving, whispering, coughing. The recorder crawls up and begins to write down a wave-like curve. Leonid glances at the device, and says,

"Well, that'll do for the first time!"

He seems to be off: his look is back to normal and good, his facial features are smoothed out; there is a smile on his lips. The arrow of the recorder hesitated for half a minute and dropped down to its initial value.

"Well, congratulations, this is the start. Now there's something to do", the head of the laboratory gets up and pats me on the shoulder.

"Now you owe us. Run to the shop and let the girls make some snack. We should celebrate this!"

It has worked. Everybody is happy. Another month or so of the experiments, and we can arrange a new stage of work, receive new funding for another year of work, and above all, begin an exciting new phase of research.

After a series of experiments with different operators I started a 24-hour operation: the power supply was stable and controlled by the devices. The recorder continuously, 24 hours a day, was writing the curve of the sensor signal. The device was placed in a separate room and did not require any special maintenance. Twice a day there was the control of parameters and data reading. In the center 5-6 operators were constantly working. Each of them was allocated a 3-hour period of time. During this time the psychic could come into the room with the equipment and practice watching the indications of the recorder. Or, I would work at a distance, noting the time of their work. Or, he would work at a distance, noting the time of his work. Then the marked moments of the impact were compared with the data of the recorder, and a conclusion was made about the presence or absence of impact and its value by a ten-point scale (Fig. 34).

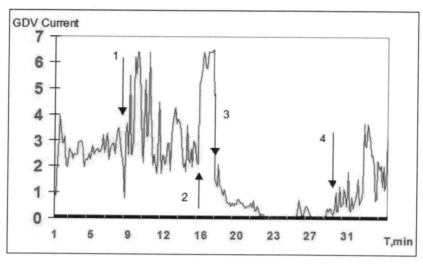

Fig.34. Time dynamics of a sensor records. 1 – beginning of the influence; 2 – feeling of Love; 3 – simulation of a death state; 4 – "coming back to life".

This technique gave us independence from the actions of the researcher, the factor that should always be considered when conducting experiments with people. Nothing exerted pressure on the operators, as well: they could work at a convenient time without any nobody's supervision and control. These working conditions suited me quite well: during the day I could spend some time in the park with a scientific journal in my hands, and at night to process the curves of the recorder. Night is the most productive time for thinking and research activities.

After two weeks of work it became clear that different operators had different effects on the sensor. The leader was a 40-year-old doctor from the suburbs of Moscow, Igor, he was followed by a nice-looking "witch" (as she called herself), Nellie from St. Petersburg; the effectiveness of the rest was significantly lower. One evening we gathered the entire group in a large room at the large table. The discussion was at tea.

"Well, now, that you all know what this stuff in an iron box is like, let's discuss how each of you treats it", I began. "Igor, yours is the greatest efficiency, will you share your experience?"

"When I'm affecting the sensor, first of all, I imagine that it is part of my body. Generally, it is the continuation of my arm. Then I start moving the energy, as I usually do when working with patients. I raise the energy level in my hands. As soon as I feel that it is under control, I can control it at will. Distance does not matter. Irrespective, whether it is from three meters or three kilometers. I specifically tested it".

"And how long can you keep this state?"

"Most important is to enter it. Then it will last. You are already in the stream. You can do something. Get distracted. The main thing is not to be emotionally involved. Emotions distract.

"And what do you feel in this state?"

"It's hard to explain. It's like swimming in warm water. Feeling that you are in the flow. And when you go out, it is a very pleasant relaxed state

"Well, thank you. Nellie, what do you say?"

"I simply love it, your sensor. It is for me like a warm kitten, gentle and affectionate. I picked keys for it for a long time: I imagined it part of myself, and read it poems, and tried to give it commands. And then I realized that I need just to love it a little.

"Like a man or like a child?" asked somebody.

"It doesn't matter however. If you love, you just love. It's the same feeling. It does not distinguish age, appearance or habits of your favorite. This feeling fills all around, as the ocean water. It dissolves you completely, you forget about yourself, and it is only important that your loved one feels well.

"How is it possible to feel so about a dead piece of iron?" wondered the girl called Nina.

"But why dead? When Konstantin made it, he put his heart into it. Thus it responds!"

"I wonder if it is possible to have a mass production of sensors labeled "0.1% heart", "0.4% heart" and put the price accordingly!' said Igor.

Everybody burst out laughing.

After this discussion "the technology of love" was accepted by all operators. And the results became much more stable. Naturally, different operators had different results. After lunch the efficiency decreased. And the same was also observed on Mondays. What was the reason? We worked seven days a week not to lose precious time. By late summer convincing statistical data on the effect of operators on the gas discharge sensor had been collected. As it was found later, a similar sensor had been tested at the same time in the United States by a team led by William Tiller[6]. That is what synchronicity of events means! At that time we were unaware of each other! In the history of science it has repeatedly observed that good ideas often come to mind of different people simultaneously. So it was with the discovery of the radio, telephone, X-ray machine and tomography. The main thing is that society must be ready for these ideas.

The next step was to work out the selectivity: whether an operator could affect a specific sensor placed next to two similar ones.

By the autumn we had returned into the city, reported the results to several commissions and got an approval to continue the experiments. During the cold winter it was necessary to improve the equipment, check out some more designs and to try to work with water and body fluids.

By that time we had had a great experience working with microbial cultures. Within a few years we managed to develop a method for determining the state of microbial cultures during cultivation. The methodology was based on using single voltage pulses and recording the glow in narrow spectral bands by using photomultiplier tubes with filters.

The main driving force of those works was Galina, the talented biophysicist with feverish energy. In the Soviet times she successfully defended her thesis on the subject, and then continued to work

---

[6] Tiller W. A gas Discharge Device for Investigating Focused Human Attention. J Sci Exploration, 1990. V. 4. №. 2.

actively. But then Perestroika began, it seemed that nobody needed scientific research; the very survival was becoming an art, and, having not stood all these complexities, Galina went to live in Germany for a quiet, tranquil existence. The method for studying microbial cultures gas-discharge method is waiting for its next enthusiast.

Having acquired the experience, we decided to find out how operators can influence biological fluids. For the experiments blood and DNA solution were selected. They were tested in the experiment. Something worked. We began to prepare the setups for a comprehensive analysis of liquids: ESR, pH, biological activity, gas discharge glow. Naturally, in addition to these experiments we had a lot of other activities and trends in research.

The next summer we again spent in the Baltics, at the retreat. It was a very interesting time: experiments, the joy of creativity when all that had been conceived came true, and you can immediately see the next step. There were seminars discussing issues ranging from experimental techniques to the philosophy of religion. Interesting people who came from across the country to share experiences, to work together to show their technique. During that time I managed to get some intensive training and learn various techniques of controlling bioenergy, both of my own and that of the environment.

In general, we have found that mental effects on physical systems are possible. Both technical and biological. To do this, first of all, we need careful selection of operators and their training. As we now call it, for the effective operation the operator should transit into an altered state of consciousness (ASC). Later we will touch upon this issue in more detail. Not everyone can do so, and the effectiveness is completely different. Like with musicians, they need talent and many years of hard work, after which it becomes clear whether the person can claim to be in the symphony orchestra or start a concert career. Without hard work professional activity is impossible. Working with energy and information is no exception. Years of hard training based on the original talent are required.

After analyses of all results obtained during the summer we saw that even with the best operators the efficiency was 70-80%. On some days it increased to 100% of the effect, on others sharply decreased. Who knows what the reason was? We were unable to find any specific correlations. It became obvious that before practical use many years of hard work were still required. With that we went back to Petersburg and sat down to write reports.

Apparently, the authorities did not like our findings. Everyone wanted a quick effect, triumphant reports, and orders on jackets. When it became clear that the work would take much time, and the ultimate prospect was very obscure, the question of the continuation of works was suspended. Moreover, the changes came: Leonid Brezhnev died, at the funerals the coffin with his body was awkwardly dropped into the grave, and superstitious people immediately took this as a special omen. Then there was a short period when the elderly colleagues of Brezhnev, one after another tried to grab the reins of power, but then left, then swept away either by a disease, or by enemies, and, eventually, the Secretary of the Regional Committee of the Communist Party Mikhail Gorbachev came to power.

During all these changes the authorities became disinterested in discovering new patterns of life; our studies terminated one after the other, and all staff members quietly resigned. Some changes seemed to be coming to the Soviet society, but nobody in the world could conceive their scale.

THE INFLUENCE OF CONSCIOUSNESS ON MATTER

Brain is an apparatus with which
we think that we think.

Ambrose Bierce (1842-1914)

The question of whether the human mind can directly, without some intermediate elements, influence the world around us has troubled mankind since ancient times. This effect is described in countless myths, legends and fairy tales of all peoples. In XX century this question arose on the new plane when the concept of the "observer" on whose conscious actions the outcome of subatomic events depended was introduced in quantum mechanics. Such interpretation is not universally accepted by physicists but it provides a theoretical foundation for study of these phenomena.

It is interesting to note that in techniques, especially in computer sciences, there is a common opinion that there are experimenters in whose hands any instrument works, and there are people negatively affecting the equipment. The first were Lord Kelvin, Thomas Edison and Nikola Tesla. The latter are usually theorists. A famous physicist George Gamow humorously describes the so-called "Pauli effect"[7]:

"It is well known that theoretical physicists are very awkward in handling experimental apparatus; and furthermore, the level of physicist - theorist can be assessed by his ability to break a delicate instrument byt simply touching it. According to this criterion, Wolfgang Pauli was an outstanding theoretician; the equipment broke, fell, blocked or burned as soon as he entered the lab".

Naturally, this is a joke, and such influence is not exerted by all theorists, but as with every joke, there is a large element of truth there.

Experiments on mental impact on random events have been conducted since the 30-ies of XX century. Classical example of such studies was the influence on the figures falling out when throwing dice. To master this ability is the dream of any casino gambler! The meta-analysis of similar data obtained from 1935 to 1987 was carried out.

---

[7] Gamow G., 1959. The exclusive principle. Scientific American, 201: 74-86

2569 people took part in the experiments trying to mentally affect 2. 6 million tosses of dice in 148 sessions with 150 000 control throws without mental effect. In the control throws the probability of accidental fall-outs was 50. 05%, while over the whole data set under influence the probability was 51.2%. It is not so much, so do not expect similar effects when playing at a casino, but it is enough to prove the existence of the effect. The enormous statistical significance of the obtained data should be taken into account![19]

Further these studies were performed on modern scientific basis with the use of electronic generators of random numbers and computer processing. The great work is carried out in U.S.; in recent years with the involvement of colleagues from other countries, mostly from Germany. The results vary from laboratory to laboratory, from year to year, showing from 49 to 53%. It turns out that there are many factors that are identifiable and mostly getting away from the understanding having a positive or a blocking effect on the outcome of the experiment[8].

In general, there is doubt that mind can influence the course of random or quasi-random processes, but this effect is generally small and elusive, it can be seen only looking very closely at the surrounding reality, or in the formulation of specific experiments.

In recent years, an interesting modification of the experiments on the influence of consciousness on physical processes was proposed by a team led by William Tiller. He is a well-known physicist, a former Dean of a faculty at Stanford University in the U.S. In parallel with the basics of work he has been always interested in research of the abnormal or borderline phenomena related to human consciousness. In particular, he studied Kirlian photography and has published several interesting articles in this area that have not lost their value up till now[21]. I've met several times with W. Tiller and we spent a few hours together having good time and discussing the prospects for development of works of the frontier science.

---

[8]   Jahn R. G., Dunne B. J. 1988. *Margins of Reality.* A Harvest/HBJ Book. San Diego, NY, London.

After his retirement in 1998, William Tiller began a series of very interesting experiments[9]. A specially selected group of psychics mentally affected a high-frequency generator made under the guidance of Professor William Tiller. After that the device was wrapped into foil and stored in the laboratory, or transported to another place. When a vessel of water was placed near the device there was a significant change in PH of the water. The design of these experiments is described in detail, they have been successfully reproduced, and W. Tiller proposed a hypothetical model where human consciousness is included as part of the material world. Note, that in most experiments, W. Tiller has used a group effect on the device. In recent years more and more evidence have been accumulated about the timing of the mental effort of a group of people that brings significant impacts on the material world.

This hypothesis was specifically tested by a well-known researcher Dean Radin in 1995-1996. He recorded the activity of an electronic generator of random numbers (RNG) in the control periods of time and during the periods when most of the American population watched emotionally meaningful television programs, such as Oscars, the final football championship, or the court verdict of the famous athlete O. Simpson. In dozens sessions of this kind there have been recorded significant changes in the RNG signal as compared with the control ones. This once again confirms the fact that our emotions are an active force of the material world! And, most surprising, not only our human emotions, but emotions of animals and birds as well, even those seemingly mindless, like chickens.

A group of French researchers led by R. Peoc'h [10] carried out a series of amazing experiences. They designed a robot that could move around without bumping into obstacles. If the robot is programmed to move at random it is moving chaotically, accidentally turning in different directions. In the room tracking sensors are placed, and after some time the trajectory of the robot uniformly fills in all available space. After that several cages with chickens are placed into the room,

---

[9] Tiller W., Dibble W., Kohane M. Exploring Robust Interactions Between Human Intention and Inanimate / Animate Systems. Frontier Perspectives. 2000. V. 9. № 2. P. 6-21; 2001. V. 10. № 1. P. 9-18.
[10] R. Peoc'h. Psychokinetic Action of Yang Chicks on the Path of an Illuminated Source. J Sci Exploration, 1995. V. 9. № 2.

and the light is turned off. Then the robot is switched on, a small bulb being mounted on it. The robot starts to randomly move around the room, but after a while it turns out that the trajectory of its motion shifts toward the cages with the chickens! That is, the chicks, stretching toward the light, seem to attract the robot by the force of their emotions!

A similar phenomenon occurs when the robot is carried before the cage with the newly hatched chickens. They take it for mom, and are ready to obediently follow him. But when the freedom of movement is limited by the cage, they call the robot-mom with all the passion of their chicken heart. And the robot obeys! It responds and begins to walk close to chicken cages. Similar results have been repeatedly reproduced and described in detail in the scientific literature.

Thus, emotions affect even an electronic machine. The question is: what is the mechanism of this influence? I am afraid that at this stage we are very far from the answer. Now our task is to accumulate experimental data and let us not hurry with conclusions.

QUANTUM BREAKTHROUGH

Nobody understands quantum theory.

Richard Feynman (1918-1988)

In recent years experimental data appeared that provided a serious scientific basis for all the above phenomena. This is an experimental justification of the so-called Einstein-Podolsky-Rosen (EPR) paradox. As we know, the great Einstein until the end of his life could not accept quantum mechanics. It seemed to him a too formal simplification of reality. He lamented, "For fifty years I've been thinking about what is a light quantum, and can not understand it, and now at the universities every Tom thinks he knows it, but he is mistaken". Einstein could not accept the probabilistic principle being the basis of quantum mechanics. He did not want to lose the certainty and truth. "God does not play dice", he said. Einstein called quantum mechanics absurd. He believed that physicists simply do not yet know the values of some hidden variables, which would allow escaping the uncertainty. Niels Bohr who opposed him believed that the probabilistic nature of the predictions of quantum mechanics can not be fundamentally eliminated. Einstein was not alone in his belief (few people would lose faith in the existence of objective reality).

In particular, from the laws of quantum mechanics it follows that no two particles belonging to a single quantum system can have the same values of quantum numbers. Therefore, if an atom emits two photons, their polarization will always be different. Now imagine, Einstein said, that these photons are emitted in different directions, and one of the photons is affected, which changes its polarization. But photons belong to the same quantum system! Hence, the polarization of the second photon must immediately change, even if it is in another part of the Universe! But this is non-contact interaction, telepathy, teleportation! "But this is impossible in nature", said Einstein. In 1935 Einstein, together with Boris Podolsky and Nathan Rosen, wrote an article entitled "Can we consider the quantum-mechanical description of physical reality complete?" where he described a virtual experiment that was subsequently named Einstein-Podolsky-Rosen (EPR) paradox which for decades remained a mystery of quantum mechanics.

After the publication of this article Niels Bohr published a paper with the same name, in which he set forth several arguments for the probabilistic description of quantum mechanics and a certain analogy between the provisions of quantum mechanics and Einstein's general theory of relativity. Thus Bohr-Einstein debate about the physical meaning of the wave function was born.

In 1951 D. Bohm considered the possibility of carrying out an experiment (technically not yet feasible at that time), the so-called optical version of the EPR experiment that could resolve the dispute of Einstein-Bohr.

Much later, in the 60-ies, John Bell pondered over the EPR paradox. He figured out how to put an end to this endless argument of physicists initiated by Bohr and Einstein. Based on the arguments of the EPR, he formalized this argument as an inequality, which is called Bell's theorem. After that he only needed to carry out the experiment. If the experiment of Bell's inequality was confirmed, Einstein was right, if not, it was Bohr. Technically, such an experiment in the 60-ies was not feasible. But at least he knew exactly what to test, what he would obtain by this check and that this check was possible in principle.

In 1982 the scientific world was excited by the report on experimental confirmation of the EPR effect. The research team led by Alain Aspect at the University in Paris presented an experiment that might prove to be one of the most significant in XX century. A. Aspect and his team discovered that under certain conditions the elementary particles, such as electrons, **are able to instantaneously communicate with each other regardless of the distance between them.** It does not matter whether there are 10 feet between them or 10 billion miles. Somehow **each particle always knows what the other one is doing.** The problem of this discovery is that it **violates the postulate of Einstein about the limiting velocity of propagation of interaction** equal to the velocity of light. Since a travel faster than the light velocity is equivalent to overcoming the time barrier, this daunting prospect made some physicists try to explain the experiments of Aspect by complicated detours.

The result caused no doubt because it was confirmed by the scientists from three different centers: Anton Zeilinger from Austrian Center in Innsbruck, Francesco Martini from Rome and Jeff Kimble from California. Technically it is a super-complex experiment. The duration of each light pulse was equal to a second in the degree of minus 15: 10^{-15}! It is impossible to imagine with one's mind. However it turned out that in every fourth case the properties of the photons from the source A coincided with the properties of the photons from the source B. This is teleportation with a probability of 25%, which was predicted in advance by the theory of EPR. In 1999 teleportation of not individual photons but of the whole beam of photons, i.e. a light beam was successfully performed.

"The most important outcome of these experiments is that they made it possible to see the amazing properties of quantum mechanics and to understand that nature follows its predictions, even when these predictions seem to be mad".

These experiments put an end to the endless disputes. Let me quote another famous physicist Paul Davies:

"The results left no doubt: Einstein was wrong. Quantum uncertainty can not be avoided. It is an integral feature of the quantum world and can not be reduced to something else. The naive view of the reality of particles with well-defined properties in the absence of observations failed.

A. Aspect hammered the final nail in the coffin of physics based on common sense".

These costly experiments are not just entertainments of highbrow scholars. The possibility of ultra-fast data transmission means a new era in the information technologies which already have their name: quantum computing. The prospects lie in the transition from electronic computers and data transmission systems to the photonic ones. Light beams have been already firmly established in the practice of data transmission through fiber optic cables, and it provided a significant increase in the capacity of communication channels. The next phase is the transition to photonic devices in the computer chips, and, finally to the use of quantum states as bits of information. This will be the next phase of technological revolution, a new leap over the coil of the information spiral.

But what about teleportation of material objects, an instantaneous transfer of bodies to another point in space, the cherished dream of all the magi? In principle, there are no restrictions to the implementation of these processes from the viewpoint of modern physics. Professor Jeff Kimble of Californian Technological University said that quantum teleportation of material objects is not far off. True, it is better not to mention biological objects at this point.

Quantum teleportation, in contrast to that described by science fiction, takes place in four stages: reading the original object, splitting the object and encoding its information, transmission of the code to a place of "assembly", and its re-establishment in the new place. Sadly, quantum teleportation is not suitable to move people from one place to another: first of all, because data processing and their interpretation is incomparably longer than a few thousandths of a second, which retain the connection between the point of assembly and disassembly even in the best experiments. For this reason the probability that a copy will be similar to the original decreases to very high-risk values.

The EPR effect provides a theoretical basis for non-contact interactions. We need only to assume that our consciousness operates on quantum principles. But this assumption is reasonable and justified. In modern computers 0 and 1 are used as bit information related to the polarization of semiconductor domains. The EPR effect opens up the prospect of encoding information by quantum states of atoms. So, can it be that our minds operate on this principle? And then it becomes evident that all phenomena in the universe are interconnected, that the ancient principle "what beneath is above" gets a new rationale, and we have another thread that leads through the labyrinth of cognition to the shining horizons of the new knowledge.

In scientific language these phenomena are called quantum entanglement; a quantum-mechanical phenomenon when the quantum state of two or more objects must be described in interaction with each other, even if individual objects are separated in space. Consequently, correlations occur between the observed physical properties of the objects. For example, it is possible prepare two particles that are in a single quantum state, so that when one particle is observed in the spin state directed upward, the spin of the other one is directed downward, and vice versa; and this is so despite quantum mechanics, according to which it is impossible to predict what directions will actually be. In other words, there is an impression that measurements of one system have an instantaneous and non-local effect on the related system (as physicists say, the systems are entangled). However what is understood as information in classical meaning can not be transmitted through the non-locality faster than with the speed of light. From the theoretical and philosophical viewpoint, this phenomenon is one of the most revolutionary properties of the quantum theory, since it is possible to see that correlations predicted by quantum mechanics are absolutely incompatible with the ideas of the seemingly apparent locality of the real world, according to which the information about the state of a system can be transmitted only by its nearest surroundings.

EXTRASENSORY INDIVIDUALS, HEALERS, BIOENERGOTHERAPISTS...

When people are taught not what they should think, but how they should think, then any misunderstanding will disappear.

Georg Chistoph Lichtenberg (1742-1799)

Being present at meetings of a community of natural scientists, I have arrived at the idea that to record the influence of human consciousness on the physical world it is necessary to try various physical systems. If people can influence each other and communicate with animals under certain conditions, they probably can influence physical processes of the world. All fairy tales and legends tell us about it. Just looked at the cake, and it will jump into your mouth.

Since then, for almost thirty years I have had to face, communicate and work with people who are involved in extrasensory practices. These people are not only Russian, but also from other different countries. Basically it is professional work. We have developed a whole set of devices for recording human abilities to influence the material world processes, and the use of this equipment enables us to reveal the levels of human abilities of non-conventional influences. Supervising all these people and a long-term experimental work have led me to the whole system of conclusions which, of course, are not definitive, but help to formulate the concept of how it all can occur and how it is connected with the people involved in the process.

First, the ability of the person for extrasensory, for healing, is a gift, a talent which is given from birth. It can be shown at various ages, it can be bred, trained; it is the same gift, as the gift of a musician, an artist, a scientist or a writer. It is a talent, and as any talent it can be manifested and developed, or can remain hidden and absolutely not known either to its owner, or people around him.

Indeed, if somewhere in Africa in a tribe of cattlemen a boy with ingenious abilities to mathematics is born, the maximum manifestation of this talent will be counting sheep in the tribe herds. If a child has the ability to music but in his childhood nobody teaches

203

him to play the violin or the piano, this ability remains non-realized, and he will be capable to sing songs heard on the radio. The same applies to a talent for influence. For realization of a talent primary ability and work are needed. Therefore all outstanding and successful psychics I met are first of all people who work much, read a lot of literature and are engaged in self-improvement; who are always training and only thanks to all these their talent gets development.

Often there rises the question, how much this talent is connected with spirituality, with moral image, with high aspirations of the person. From my point of view, there is no connection at all. Just as a talent of a musician, an artist or a writer is a special gift which has no relation to the personality of its owner. Thus, as **Russian poet A.S. Pushkin** ingeniously noticed, this gift can be shown only in special conditions.

> Until he hears Apollo's call
> To make a hallowed sacrifice,
> A Poet lives in feeble thrall
> To people's empty vanities;
> And silent is his sacred lyre,
> His soul partakes of chilly sleep,
> And of the world's unworthy sons
> He is, perhaps, the very least.
> But once Divinity's command
> Approaches his exquisite ear,
> The poet's soul awakens, poised,
> Just like an eagle stirred from sleep.
> All worldly pleasures leave him cold,
> From common talk he stays aloof,
> And will not lower his proud head
> Before the nation's sacred cow.
> Untamed and brooding, he takes flight,
> Seething with sound and agitation,
> To reach a sea-swept, desert shore,
> A woodland wide and murmuring...

In the same way it is with an energy therapist. I happened to meet talented psychics who had the strongest influence on other people being absolutely immoral, stupid and cold. I remember a vivid example that I came across with many years ago. Once with a group of our scientists and psychics we went to a large conference to a country of palm trees, ocean beaches and elephants. In our group there was one lady, let's call her Galina. She worked in a northern Russian city where she enjoyed enormous popularity and the support of the mayor; she had her office in a polyclinic, and patients lined up to it several months in advance, and, as I understood, she was really able to render real help. It is enough to say that during 4 days of our stay on that island she could completely relieve the spouse of the Russian Consul of migraines, pains in the back and sharply improved her general state. When Galina was engaged in healing she came into an Altered State of Consciousness, and the return into the usual condition demanded big time. One evening we were having supper at the hotel; before that Galina had worked with patients and as it often happens to healers, it was very difficult for her to stop, leave the special state which was supported automatically, irrespective of the person's desire. Therefore she had to "spend" it on someone else.

We were sitting at supper, and the owner of hotel, a local man with whom we had communicated the second or third day and who, naturally, didn't speak Russian, came to sit with us. And, having looked at that man attentively, Galina said to me, "Konstantin, translate to him, please, I see that he has big problems in his life". I translated. He exclaimed, "Yes, yes, yes, really indeed. How'd you know?" "I know and I can learn all about you". "But how?" "Well, very simply. Let me tell you about your life". "Yes, yes, yes!" Galina concentrated, and then began to tell him about the episodes from his life. She told that he had grown in a poor family, they had a palm hut, that his father was a cruel and severe man and his mother was a kind, but weak woman. Father often beat him. "I even see a scourge on the wall with which he beat you". The owner of the hotel nodded, "Yes, it was so!" "And very often you escaped to the grandmother where stayed for days". "Yes, yes, yes, I did". "And the grandmother was the only person who was sorry for you and with whom you found rest. You grew a normal healthy child, but you had a foot trauma, you cut it playing football, or with a barbed wire, or with something else, and

205

you had a very bad wound". "Yes, yes, yes", and then he lifted his trouser-leg and showed a big scar on his foot.

Then she told him about traumas and illnesses which had been in his life, and further told that now there was a difficult situation connected with problems in business and with problems in his family which he also confirmed nodding his head. Then Galina said, "If you want, I can help you, I will work on you, and all this will end" "Yes, yes, of course", the owner of hotel exclaimed.

After supper we went to bed, and Galina remained with the owner in the hall and worked with him till 4 o'clock in the morning. Unfortunately, I don't know what influenced his further destiny, but, anyway, he was very happy, and when we were leaving in a week he gave Galina a remarkable gift.

This woman was really able to work, and at that time she changed, was literally shining, she told beautiful things, very correct things, she spoke about good, about love, about Christ, about mutual sacrificing, and her words made strong impression upon listeners. Though, I underline, she could influence without words, too, working with people who did not understand Russian.

That is one side of her nature. But there was also the other side. In everyday life when she was not engaged in healing and did not enter the Altered State she was one of the most stupid, silly, greedy and unpleasant women I have ever met in my life. Here are some examples. She was rather big, and one of her life hobbies was gorging. We were fed well, but basically with fruit and local eastern food with lots of seasonings and spices, and Galina did not enjoy it. Fortunately, she had taken from Moscow a pair of bags with good Russian products, and every evening she laid a table in her hotel room to eat in loneliness. One more interesting moment was connected with food. When Galina was engaged in healing for all love to food she could not eat during a whole day, or even as she said, several days, i.e. there was no need for food in the Altered State of Consciousness. She worked with people, accepted dozens visitors without eating even a crumb.

The conference was held on a fine southern island, on the coast of the Indian Ocean, and, naturally, all of us spent much time walking in the vicinities, visiting local temples or swimming in the ocean. Galina only once left the ocean coast to pose for a television cameraman. It was one of the film episodes in which she, according to her own expression, "welcomed the ocean". When she was offered to go somewhere to have a look at some beautiful views, she would always answer, "To drag somewhere in such heat? No way!" She was not interested at all. She was preoccupied only with her own affairs and problems. The only thing she showed her interest in was shopping, and the Consul took her to different places, and her greatest attention was paid to a shop where there was a sale of cheap things. There she bought several sacks of things which then she hardly managed to drag through customs. Her stinginess knew no bounds. For example, such case. The local population lives in full poverty, there is a universal unemployment, therefore everybody who has a job hold on for it at any cost. Once we were riding on a mini bus, and it is necessary to note that to drive on local roads you need a special art, because these roads are blocked by people, buffalos, elephants, cars of diversified models, and all of them walk, go, run, jump in all possible directions; so, at first sight, no traffic regulations exist. Therefore it is no surprise that somebody bumps into somebody else, but all this ends in gaining mutual understanding. And so our small bus, doing another maneuver, touched a little table of some seller. The fruit rushed down, the little table fell, the seller jumped up, shouting and gesticulating, a crowd gathered immediately. After a while the driver approached us with a very apologizing look and said,

"Could you lend me some rupees (the sum of about $5s) that I would pay off this seller and we could go further?"

Naturally, for us it was a small sum, it did not demand any discussion, but our healer jumped up from her seat and shouted, "Why should we pay for this driver? If he isn't able to drive, let him pay off for his mistakes. Why should I give my money for some swarthy?"

However Galina was not the poorest, and, besides the bags with things on the way back, she bought a ringlet with a large emerald. There was awkward silence, I took 5 dollars, gave them to the driver, and the incident was settled. There were many such cases.

All our communication showed that a gift for influencing, a gift for healing and the personality are absolutely independent. Later on such things proved to be true repeatedly. All practice of work with healers, with psychics, the practice of their experimental examination enables to divide them conditionally into some big categories.

The first category is simply charlatans; charlatans who use trustful people, and not only our Russian, but also western, eastern, Europeans, Americans, and cheat them.

Another category of healers is people who are engaged in psychotherapy. For millennia this profession has been extremely popular. In many areas of Christian religion this position belongs to clergymen, and each parishioner regularly comes and confesses his sins. But isn't confession a certain field of psychotherapy? If a priest is clever and attentive he will have a talk with the parishioner, listen to him and give a piece of advice and it will be based on thousand-year wisdom of Christian church. In XX century the role of confessors was played by doctors with professional diploma; they propagated Freud's and Jung's theories, various psychoanalytic approaches and, making use of all experience stored by science, rendered a professional psychotherapeutic help. In the West each self-esteemed person considers his duty to pay visit to his psychoanalyst once a year, or even once a month. And it really works. From outside it is always easier to see somebody's problems and troubles and on the basis of experience, books, or a simply wise foreign viewpoint to give any advice. In Russia where the practice of medical aid in this field is not developed and the church has not returned its role undermined during the decades of atheistic propagation, the role of psychotherapists was substituted by healers, the so-called psychics. Such healer will talk to the person, will allow him to speak and you know that to tell an extraneous person about problems, troubles, urgent issues is already good psychotherapy, already a good step to improvement of the state of health. And if a healer is good, he will tune the person in an optimistic way, will help him to see a wider picture of life, direct his thoughts to light, beauty, to God and this by itself will help the person to live easier, to bear all burdens and hardships of real life. Thus, such help is really real, it is necessary for many peiople, especially for many women, and it really works. It influences the state, because our state in many ways depends on how we adjust it, how we treat it and how we build our life. Therefore the given category of folk healers is popular enough and works well in the open spaces of our immense Native land.

The next type is a healer-hypnotist. As a rule, these are people acting from a stage though it is not obligatory. But among those who act showing special mental abilities most of them refer to this type. This is a person with a magic look, a person able to capture the attention of audience, able to suppress people's will, in other words, a professional practicing a form of hypnosis. And naturally, the basic working condition of such healer is selection of patients. Among people visiting such performances or sessions there are those of different degree of suggestibility, the ability of being hypnotized. And a healer-hypnotist can work only with such people. Depending on abilities, on the degree of mastering the technique, the circle of such dependable persons can be bigger or smaller, and separate professionals-virtuosos with this special gift have a very wide circle of such patients. Certain objective of the improvement of state of health, of the change of the general spirit, of the change of the attitude to life is created, which starts to work further independently and to have a positive effect.

Once, academician Natalya Bekhtereva (who recently died) had told the following story. After a meeting with Kashpirovsky they went to a restaurant. They started to study the menu, and then Kashpirovsky said, "Dear Natalya Petrovna, with your bodily constitution you should eat only light salads. Let me set forth an objective and you won't feel hungry for a long time".

N. P. Bekhtereva was amazed, shocked, and somewhat revolted. The statement was unexpected and tactless. But she did not want to spoil the evening; therefore she tried to make a joke, "Thanks, the respected, but it is already rather late for me to change my habits. I prefer to suffer at a festive table more rather than to enjoy a bread crust in a desert".

But when appetizers were served, N. P. Bekhtereva suddenly felt no more appetite. It was gone. "Can it be that it works?" she asked herself, "No, I will be stronger", and she forced herself to eat both appetizers, and the first course, and the second. After a while the appetite appeared again.

The next level is healers using various physiotherapeutic methods of influence and national techniques. These are different kinds of massage, traditional and energy, point and Oriental, the use of various herbs, tinctures, natural preparations, and physiotherapy and acupuncture methods. All these methods are to some extent effective, though, of course, the result depends on the professionalism of a doctor or healer. And if they are used in combination with modern techniques with estimation of the human state and the control of the course of treatment such approaches can be very effective. And, finally, there are rare professionals who can influence the material world phenomena with their Consciousness. These phenomena can be electronic avalanches of gas discharge in the special sensor, molecular clusters in potable water, or physiological processes in the human body. In all cases there are changes of the state of the investigated system under the influence of a strong-willed effort of another person. These changes can be recorded by objective methods; hence, they can be a subject of scientific research.

How to distinguish healers of one level from psychics of another? In their advertising they all tell about the guaranteed treatment from all illnesses, so it seems even strange: why do people continue to crowd in polyclinics and to swallow tablets? They are probably fools. Well, and if it is serious, then as in any profession, there should be methods of objective testing and control in extrasensory practice. And such methods have been developed, in particular, at our laboratory.

A TEST FOR A PSYCHIC

> *Science is the belief in the ignorance of the experts.*
>
> *Richard Feynman (1918-1988)*

By mid-90ies in Russia there was a large quantity of psychics-healers. The state medicine was in a deep crisis; the absence of financing sharply aggravated the problems that exist in classical medicine all over the world. Medical products did not suffice. Hospitals collapsed. Doctors drank. And the people began to address folk healers. Or those who called themselves that way. At every corner there were signboards: "Cooperative society the Healer. Will help you to recover from any illness". For such activity in those years neither licenses, nor diplomas were required, only payment of minimum taxes. In certain cases similar activity was really effective. The percent of the cured depended on the concrete healer and could be hardly reasonably accounted. In many cases it was simply conscious or unconscious cheating. But in those days there were enough patients.

Gradually many serious people have come to understanding of the necessity of ordering such activity. But how? To trust diplomas of healer schools? But none of these schools had a state status, and such scientific discipline at that time did not exist. And, first of all, there were no criteria of estimating extrasensory influences. Certainly, the first and the main criterion is the state of the patient. Whether or not he feels better after a session. However here interferes the effect of a placebo, the effect of auto-suggestion. Conviction in a positive effect of treatment in most cases leads to improvement of the human state. Especially, it would be desirable to believe that money has been spent but not wasted. It is a very useful effect for the patient, but it can be not connected in any way with the influence of the healer. It is necessary to estimate the magician. And without the patients being involved. Such kind of experiments with people is not quite ethic. Even if they voluntary agree. And what if the influence will appear harmful? Nobody can predict it in advance. And patients may not be able to suspect about it.

Thus, in the society there was a social order: to develop methods of testing psychics. This issue was supported by a group of initiative people at the level of the Ministry of Health and even the State Parliament. We have appeared to get involved in this work, though without money, but with prospects of financing which, alas, was never realized.

We have developed a special device which was very sensitive to change of mental state of the subjects. By means of a special sensor the signal was recorded from one or several fingers. In the beginning the signal curve was measured in its initial condition to determine the borders of background changes; then the subject was given a task to change his or her state.

When modeling strong emotional conditions, sincere praying, or during meditation the readings confidently changed. If the person didn't change the condition but only pretended, the signal remained almost constant. The first experiments with strong healers showed that when they modeled an influence condition on the patient, the signal changed considerably.

Thus, in our arsenal there was a variety of the following instrument techniques:

- a GDV-bioelectrography device for determining the initial state and the level of the subject's health, and a possibility of a strong-willed change of the glow area of fingers;

- the device for recording the dynamic curves in the course of modeling healing;

- gas discharge sensor.

We also added two more tests:

- definition of alive/dead by a photo;

- the test for magnetic field

The latter was carried out in the following way: in five identical wooden boxes electromagnets were placed. It was necessary to define which of them was switched on at the current moment.

The results of each of these tests were estimated in points from 0 to 10, so the possible maximum was 50 points. We checked up the system of tests on ourselves and friends; then I called some healer centers and invited their employees to come to us and test their abilities. By that time our studies of the Kirlian effect had been known widely enough: articles in a number of journals had been published; we had regularly participated in conferences. Therefore without any announcements psychics started arriving at the Center. We held testing and gave the certificates where the results were fairly described. As far as I know, further these certificates were used by many of them when they needed certification. Within two years we tested more than 150 people who claimed for abilities to work with bioenergy. The result was unexpected. About a third of them had less than 20 points, i.e. no special results. Another third gained up to 40 points, which can be achieved after some auto-training or by bioenergy methods. And less than 40 people showed really interesting results, inexplicable by a simple variation of parameters. From these 40 a group of 9 persons was chosen including a number of popular healers, among them were Alan Chumak, Alexey Nikitin, Victor Filippi and Albert Ignatenko. The 9 persons were less than 6 % from the total number of the surveyed and during all tests they got the highest points, i.e. they could influence both sensors and water, and successfully enough detect the switched on magnetic field.

THE ENERGY OF CONSCIOUSNESS

However even the high points received by these certainly talented people are not their guarantee of 100 % efficiency in all cases. It was obvious from our experiments. Like all other people they have good and bad days, they have everyday problems and physical indispositions. Besides, for all professionalism there are situations they are not able to handle. So it is necessary to treat their statements with accuracy.

Well, of course, the number of charlatans, rascals and swindlers among the so-called "psychics" surpasses all possible norms. Recently the activities of Grigory Grabovoy gained a wide popularity. With his powerful charisma, he managed to attract big groups of his followers who were ready to spend considerable money for his services. A day of group training at his seminars gathering hundreds of people cost 2 thousand roubles (about 60 euros by the prices of that time), while individual training cost more than 1000 euros. Healer sessions cost the same. Were they effective? Nobody knows. In case of such mass actions the law of the big numbers, or the law of the network marketing works, when a competently organized company on the basis of NLP (neuro-linguistic programming) helps to convince people in the justice of absolutely absurd statements.

Grabovoy developed his activity all over the country and this helped him to create a powerful financial corporation, involving more and more zombied adherents, publishing books, making films and brochures. It would have proceeded for many years, but the maestro was ruined by pride. Or else, by a demon who, having involved him in this activity and in due course was bored and decided to have some fun. Grabovoy decided that he was absolutely all-powerful, and could raise people from the dead. Full absurdity! But the trouble was that people trusted him. And brought big money to the Field of Fools. Naturally, nobody was revived and did not get out of the grave, but nobody from dozens (and maybe hundreds) of the cheated people addressed the authorities.

Nobody knows how long would last that devilish sabbath but Grabovoy trespassed all borders of cynicism and immorality. He declared that he could raise the dead who had perished in Beslan, and demanded from the unfortunate parents 37 thousand roubles for each lost child.

That was too much! The public rose against Grabovoy; he was prosecuted for swindling, and arrested.

Naturally, the first stage was a psychiatric examination. It would be desirable to believe that a normal person could not reach such lawlessness. Experts recognized Grabovoy absolutely sane. Then the investigation began that proceeded for many months.

On June 7th, 2008 the Judge of Tagansky Court of Moscow Elena Ivanova made the decision: the Court sentenced the pseudo-healer Grigory Grabovoy to 11 years of imprisonment in a standard regime penal colony, to the penalty of 1 million roubles in favor of the state and to paying 37 thousand roubles to each of the seven victims who had addressed in court.

Such decision can be welcomed. Not to mention how many people were deceived by pseudo-healers promising a fast recovery of deadly illnesses, there are moral limits to cynicism. To earn money using people's grief, impudently deceiving them and playing with the most sacred feelings is a crime that should be punished with all severity of the law, like theft and robbery. Until similar robbers plunder the trustful population, all healing activities will be the object of criticism and attacks. And it will continue until testing and licensing of the healer activity is introduced. Just as it is in any other trade.

As to the modern attitude to a mighty tribe of the Russian psychics, the technique of their testing, approved and proved, was not claimed by the ministries. Others winds blew, the officials were replaced, and the problem of ranging healers ceased to be urgent. Basically, it could be solved at the level of personal contacts, but since last years I had acquired strong idiosyncrasy to the ministerial thresholds, and was looking forward to new interesting problems. So we curtailed the program of testing and moved further. One of the subjects we always were interested in and with which we periodically experimented was a distant transfer of emotions, a kind of telepathy. This seemingly exotic ability is inherent in many people though not all are aware of it and not all use it consciously. Naturally, this property is directly connected with the level of development of intuition.

INSTEAD OF THE EPILOGUE:
TO BELIEVE OR NOT TO BELIEVE?

> *The first mouthful from the cup of natural*
> *sciences generates atheism, but at the bottom*
> *of the vessel we will find God.*
>
> *Verner Gejzenberg (1901-1976)*

If you, dear reader, have reached this page, it means that you have read the most part of the book. And many have the right question to ask: is it possible to believe everything what the author has written? To what extent should I trust this information? This question arises periodically. I am often asked, "Do you trust in homeopathy? In acupuncture? In life on Mars?" To which I always answer, "I trust only in the Lord and in my family. All other things should be checked".

The words I "trust", I "believe" have the meaning of unconditional trust. All our life is constructed on trust. We trust our life and health to the doctor, hoping that he is competent and skilled enough. We trust sellers and manufacturers, going to the shop to buy food. We trust the knowledge which we are taught at school and which is published in textbooks and guidebooks. None of us thinks of reproducing numerous experiences being the basis of modern physics, chemistry and biology. A gentle kid trustfully stretches his hand to you, he is completely in your power, completely depends on you, you are a unique source of life for him. He trusts your each word, believes everything that surrounds him, and many years will pass before he understands how much deception, lies and contradictions are around.

To find the golden mean between a thoughtless trust of the kid and an eternal doubt of the Doubtful Thomas is a challenge. The waves of the information, propagation, and advertising fall upon us, from which it is necessary to choose what to trust and what to reject. It is important both in an everyday life, and in a science.

In late XIX century a young student came to a known physicist and told that he wanted to study theoretical physics. "Young man, don't

215

waste your life", the master answered. "The building of physics has been constructed. It is beautiful and firm. There remained only small stains in dark corners".

That young student was Max Planck, one of geniuses of the science of XX century, the founder of nuclear physics. It was good for him not to obey the master and not to be engaged in banking. This is a vivid example of that the most recognized authorities only reflect representations of their circle, which are not always true. And where is the truth? Is it in science? The science is an art of construction of models which to some extent reflect the processes occurring in nature. People accept these models for real things forgetting that they are only a play of mind.

There was a model of the flat Earth and the Sun rotating round the planet. This model is quite adequate, if you need to mark a garden site or to predict the sunrise time for tomorrow. You do not need to know the radius of the Earth to do this. Then Galilei and Newton constructed the model of the Universe and the laws operating in it, and this model is absolutely adequate for a description of the surrounding reality. Only when the scientists discovered the surprising chasms of the structure of atom and an infinite quantum world, the new model of the world was needed. This quantum world does not deny Newton's world, there is transition of one into another at small velocities and big distances.

A new scientific understanding, a new paradigm wins the world only when there is a public requirement for it, when the society matures to its understanding. Darwin's theory has a number of defects, it actually doesn't explain the evolutionary process, but in XIX century it was the first theory which enabled to logically explain the formation of new species without resorting to Divine influence. Therefore it was picked up with delight and till now dominates in all biological textbooks. The description of the experiments of an Austrian monk Mendel on breeding the multi-colored peas being now the classics of genetics remained not noticed for his contemporaries, and only later was accidentally discovered in the forgotten journals.

For years the enthusiasts have been developing the automobile engines working on alternative energy sources. In 1998 in Germany I saw such engine working on water. But only when mankind has come nearer to the prospect of oil crisis the cars with hybrid engines have started to be made in the world.

Therefore, science, as well as all society, develops in stages. We can track them in the history of the western society, and now from the stage of "conquering the atom" we have come over to the epoch of Genetics and the Internet. Over the last 10 years the world has changed, we have received devices and possibilities which were difficult even to imagine, and all this is based on the achievements of modern science. Science became an active force of our society.

Now again many masters consider that the building of science is constructed. That it is beautiful and firm, and there are only small stains in dark corners. But is it really so?

None of the trends of modern science includes Consciousness in consideration. In medicine and biology this concept does not exist at all. They work with reactions, tissues, the processes proceeding in various volumes one of which is us. Psychology accurately avoids this question studying character, temperament, mutual relations of people, the place of man in the society, but not consciousness. At the same time, it is obvious that in XXI century the question "What is Consciousness?" has become one of basic for the life of our society, and gradually it starts to more and more attract the attention of scientists.

And, as in the case with quantum mechanics, the more we plunge into this world, the more of its infinity we can see. And it is only one of the examples.

On the way of cognition surprising discoveries and artful traps, ingenious insights and ridiculous deadlocks are waiting for us. What should we trust?

And again we repeat that it is necessary to treat all new ideas openly and without prejudices, but to take nothing on trust. The more difficult the research area, the more discoveries and paradoxes wait for us on the way of cognition. The new century only begins, and it is difficult even to imagine the grandeur of changes we can expect.

Now let me summarize. There is one, the most important criterion of all that we do. This criterion is the command of our heart. If a person lives according to Divine Laws, if he listens to his conscience and tries to be good to other people, life will develop more and more new surprising prospects before him. Naturally, we should bear in mind that life of each individual person is part of the collective process. Each of us is included in numerous structures, and our destiny depends on the condition of each cell of this structure, on the way of development of the whole society. We live our own life, but it is as a small nested doll enclosed in the structure of family, the working collective and all society. And all peripetias taking place in higher structures are reflected in an individual destiny. It can be said that each of us floats in his small boat along the rough river, and the current now accelerates, rushing in a rough stream through thresholds and whirlpools, now gets into quiet creeks, now spreads in a wide, free stream. We should steer the boat, trying to keep it in the middle of the river, but do we always manage to do it in the rough stream of life?

The unique well-tried remedy keeping the boat floating is Love, sensual, passionate and burning Love; gentle and timid Love; respectful and reverential Love, Love to the other person, love to children, love to the Homeland, love to the Higher Truth. This feeling seems abstract, but it absolutely specifically influences the man state, spiritualizing his life, lifting it over the routine of his daily life.

A remarkable illustration is the data presented by the researchers from Sverdlovsk E. H and V.A. Anufrievs at an international conference in Slovenia. Their objective was to measure the energy of two loving people. The two persons were in different rooms, they were asked to think about each other, and at this moment they were measured with two GDV devices. After processing the images a surprising fact was discovered! In the majority of experiments (and there were more than 20) on the images there was an impulse going from one heart to the other was! It was the energy impulse of Love! (see Fig. 27).

"Yes", my kind reader will get sad, "It is hard to understand all and not to get into a trap of the dexterous swindlers, the Fox and the Cat... What are we to do?"

First of all, let us treat all with optimism and humor. We have already argued that our life is the Fine Adventure given to us for Pleasure and Grief, Delight and Sadness, Dreams and Achievements. Don't be afraid to be trapped, don't be afraid of being ridiculous and deceived, is happens with everyone in life, and the deceiver will eventually be punished. But give it to the hands of

Divine. Live enjoying life trifles, make your holidays to celebrate little events, and periodically give vent to your emotions. But the most important thing is to live working and caring, observing the Divine Commandments and human laws. Don't try to cheat and don't wait for a freebie. Free cheese can be only in a mousetrap. If it was possible to win in a casino, they would be ruined long ago and would not spend millions for advertising. Perceive life honestly and openly, and it will give you pleasant surprises. Start to form the world round you by a positive relation to people and yourself, and you will see how after a while your desires will start to be fulfilled, as in a magic fairy tale. Only this fairy tale should be based on your real life. Good luck, and let your Aura shine even more brightly!

6319261R00119

Made in the USA
San Bernardino, CA
07 December 2013